In the Realm of the Gods

Lands, Myths, and Legends of China

Victoria Cass

Long River Press
360 Swift Avenue, Suite 48
South San Francisco, CA 94080
www.longriverpress.com

and in the People's Repubic of China by
Foreign Languages Press
24 Baiwanzhuang Rd.
Beijing 100037
www.flp.com.cn

Editors: Chris Robyn, Xu Rong
Book and Cover Design: Nathan Grover
Published in Association with Foreign Languages Press, China
The publisher wishes to thank Tommy "Shenzhenboy" Liu

Printed in China

ISBN: 978-1-59265-076-7
10 9 8 7 6 5 4 3 2 1

Library of Congress Cataloging-in-Publication Data

Cass, Victoria Baldwin.
   In the realm of the gods : lands, myths, and legends of China / Victoria Cass.
        p. cm.
   ISBN-13: 978-1-59265-076-7 (pbk.)
  1. Legends--China. I. Title.
   GR335.C345 2007
   398.20951--dc22

                                        2007024777

For Sarah and Isaac

Acknowledgments

Much of the creative inspiration for this book comes from the work of Professor Cyril Birch, a wonderful scholar and writer, whose collection of Chinese myths was published over forty years ago.

I cannot say enough about the photographers in this project. Their accomplishments are clear to see in their work. As the ad hoc editor of their art, I can attest to their magnanimity and decency. They were always a pleasure to work with. They responded happily to my requests for their work, and they were generous as hosts. From my first meeting with Chen Jianxing in Suzhou and Xiang Xiaoyang in Chongqing I was grateful for their kindness. In Shanghai Wang Rending—photographer and publisher at De Voyage Books—was both kind and generous; and the China Photographers Association in Beijing, especially Mr. Lin Tao and Mr. Hou Jianjiang, were a delight. I am very grateful as well for the help of others in China: Tao Wenyu in Suzhou, Ms Liu Yang in Chongqing, and in Beijing Ms Wang Xin at Morrison and Foerster.

In preparing the manuscript I received invaluable help from Gregg Rippey and Nathan Grover.

I would like to thank, Lynn Freed, a faithful reader whose suggestions and patience I have always valued.

I appreciate as well Rowman and Littlefield's granting me the right to use the map of China originally created by the calligrapher Tu Xinshi, and published in my previous book, *Dangerous Women, Warriors, Grannies and Geishas of the Ming*.

Of course, without the help, support, encouragement and guidance of my editor Chris Robyn this would not have been possible. I appreciate especially his work shepherding the manuscript through the stages of acceptance in China.

And, as always, I relied upon the generous help of Steve, my husband.

I would like to remind the reader that I have made a leap of faith in this book. These stories, though gathered from original Chinese sources, are not scholarly translations, but are retellings, as I have assumed the role, in this book, of storyteller.

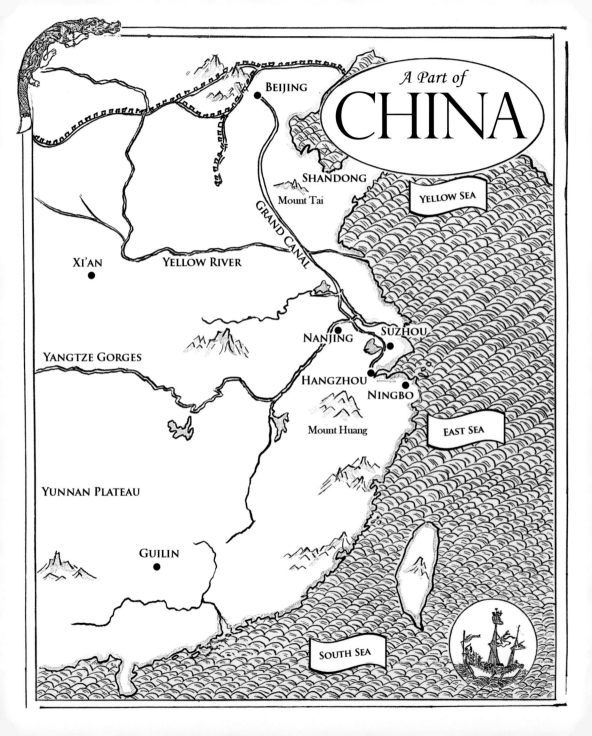

A Part of
CHINA

BEIJING

SHANDONG

Mount Tai

YELLOW SEA

XI'AN

YELLOW RIVER

GRAND CANAL

NANJING

SUZHOU

YANGTZE GORGES

HANGZHOU

NINGBO

Mount Huang

EAST SEA

YUNNAN PLATEAU

GUILIN

SOUTH SEA

Literature is the landscape that lies over my desk; landscape is the literature that lies over this earth.

~Zhang Chao, *You Meng Ying*, 17th century.

All mountains, whether large or small, contain gods and powers, and the strength of these divinities is directly proportional to the size of the mountains. In some cases when we journey into the mountains, we perceive the divinities in eerie lights and shadows and in strange sounds. A journey into these precincts requires the proper protective charm, for without one, a large tree may fall when there is no wind, or a high rock fall for no apparent reason. ...

Mountains are not to be entered lightly.

~Ge Hong, The Master Who Embraces Simplicity, 4th century

List of Chinese Dynasties

Ancient Period

Xia Dynasty 2070 B.C.-1600 B.C.

Shang Dynasty 1600 B.C– c.1046 B.C.

Zhou Dynasty c. 1046 B.C.–256 B.C.

        Spring and Autumn Period 770 B.C.-476 B.C.

Warring States Period 475 B.C.–221 B.C

        The Kingdom of Chu

        The Kingdom of Qin

        The Kingdom of Lu

        The Kingdom of Yan

The Qin Dynasty 221 B.C.–206 B.C.

Western Han Dynasty 206 B.C.–A.D. 25

Eastern Han Dynasty A.D.25–220

Medieval Period

Three Kingdoms 220–280

Jin Dynasty 265–420

Northern and Southern Dynasties 420–589

        Qi Dynasty

        Liang Dynasty

        Chen Dynasty

        Wei Dynasty

Sui Dynasty 581–618

Tang Dynasty 618–907

Five Dynasties 907–960

Late Imperial Period

    Northern Song Dynasty 960–1127

    Southern Song Dynasty 1127–1279

    Yuan, or Mongol, Dynasty 1279–1368

    Ming Dynasty 1368–1644

    Qing, or Manchu, Dynasty 1644–1911

Table of Contents

INTRODUCTION
Sacred Travelers

In the cold, long evenings of winter, Grandmother would set up the little coal brazier and my sister and brother and I would gather round it. My brother told stories, and my sister and I would listen.... He would tell us eerie tales of the strange, and act out the part of the ghost. Of course, my sister and I were easily frightened, especially when the wind came whistling through the paper-screened windows and the lamplight suddenly flickered. Then, all at once, the whole room would become off-kilter and strange, and we would scream in fright. Then my brother was delighted, and he would clap his hands with a great laugh.[1]

Yuan Zhongdao (1570-1623)

"Most of the people in my village were illiterate, but such words flew from their mouths that you'd have thought they were educated scholars. They were full of wondrous stories..."

So claims Mo Yan, one of the finest literary novelists of China. His own "Big Grandpa" was, he said, the best among the village storytellers. Without benefit of books he could spin out the infinite array of fantastic characters and terrifying settings that make a tale chilling.[2]

Big Grandpa, did, however, have some help, for if books were not his source, the landscape was. Big Grandpa could turn to the places of his village for his storylines and prompts, knowing that fantastic creatures were grounded creatures, always encountered in the same spots.

Big Grandpa gives Mo Yan an example. On one of his house calls—he was the village doctor—he runs into a watery, female, eel-demon.

> A couple of nights ago, I went over to Old Wang the Fifth's house in East Village to check on his wife. On my way back, as I passed that small stone bridge, I saw a woman in white sitting on the bridge and crying. I said to her, "Big Sister, it's the middle of the night. Why are you out here all alone, and what are you crying about?"
>
> She said, "Mister, my child is sick, he's dying. Would you go take a look at him?"
>
> My Big Grandpa said, "I know every woman in Gaomi, so this one had to have been a demon." He asked her, "Where do you live?"
>
> The woman pointed under the bridge, "There."
>
> My Big Grandpa then said, "You can't fool me. I know you're that white eel demon under the bridge."
>
> Seeing that her ploy had failed, she covered her mouth and smiled. "You've got it again!"
>
> Then, with a jerk of her head, she leaped under the bridge.

Eel demons may seem unusual in some neighborhoods, but not in the storyteller's; for bridges at night do generally accommodate watery females. Indeed, when Big Grandpa arrived at the bridge, surely, none but the youngest listener would be surprised to find a demonic woman.

Big Grandpa was simply exploiting a well-known fact of Chinese storytelling. In the huge terrain of China, legendary beings do show up when the setting calls for them. A mountain path requires the sage or mountain demon, a forest summons up a fox fairy, and the eel demon waits at night by the bridge. A monster can, when asked, provide a local address.

But when Big Grandpa drew from the well of legends, to pull out his fox fairy or snake demon, his mountain sage or divine messenger, he was not using a shallow pool of country tales. He drew, rather, from a powerful set of ancient beliefs and practices. He was recreating for Mo Yan the ancient and medieval landscape, telling him of the time when these legends were frightening or miraculous, of a time when the priest, the shamaness, the mystic, and even the Confucian intellectual, believed in the legend specific to the place, a time when they appeased the demon of the river, they prayed for rain at the mountain shrine, or entered a cave to seek the goddess.

Not that all creatures were called by the same name. The shaman of folk religions might summon a demon of the drought, the adepts of

3

Daoism might berate a demon of sickness and a Buddhist priest would decry the demon of illusion. The Chinese landscape is stratified like a geological template, with overlapping layers of religious beliefs producing sedimentary deposits specific to their proprietary gods.

Within the earliest strata of myth sits the great cauldron of folk religions, and simmering at the top is shamanism. Shamanism provided the most ancient level of land-based gods: the Divine Women of the peaks, or the River Lord of the waterways. These gods were the first of the divine landlords, fixed to place, waiting for the traveler. Daoism followed suit; it has an enormous pantheon of gods and goddesses that inhabit the landscape, from mountain precipice to back garden. And Buddhists, upon arrival from India, rapidly accommodated their worship to the sacred sites, and even stodgy Confucianism, which some think is only for urban officials, was steeped in the lore of strange places. Strange creatures of all religions came from the fissures of a landscape saturated with magic.

And if the gods were fixed to place, it was the job of the priest or priestess, exorcist or shamaness to find them. To cure a disease, release a curse, produce rain or protect a soul after death, the adept traveled to the god's address. Controlling the gods meant paying a call; and the art of magic was the art of travel. Even geomancy (or *feng shui*) follows the exorcist's path, for it too names the animate properties of the earth. This esoteric field of knowledge is the appropriation of the earth's power, a system of interpreting the phenomenon of the malign and beneficial influences generated by man's location on its ominous surface. Indeed, whatever the pantheon, whatever the theory, magicians are sacred travelers.

Fortunately, there were road maps. Daoists have left us star-travel maps and exorcists' travelogues; Confucians have described their visits to shrines. And shamanism has left us the archetypal sacred word-map, the elemental account of sacred travel. A book entitled *Shan Hai Jing* (Guideways Through Mountains and Seas) describes the shaman's divine expedition following the exorcist's path. In this book we come upon the hundreds of fantastic beings tied to place.

> The twenty-five mountains along the first guideway… from Single-Fox Mountain to Dike Mountain extend for 5,900 li. Their gods all have human faces and snakes' bodies. The proper sacrifice to them is the burial of a rooster and pig and burial of scepter for the jade offering. There is no grain offering.

Shan Hai Jing provides, helpfully, the great and familiar gods as well as a cast of minor deities and goblins, and even directions, distances, local features and helpful landmarks. It is a Michelin guide for monsters. Clearly, the exorcist needs such map-magic, as her power derives from travel over a planet that—at least for the time of the journey—becomes supernatural.

Big Grandpa, the storyteller, simply follows her path. He summons up from the landscape its monsters and spirits; he is a latter day officiant en route to the right creature at the right address.

Water

Of course, it's easy to envy Big Grandpa's strange visits: a wayside encounter could always make good material. But it was another matter all together to be the traveler by the waterside, especially in the ancient landscape. In these magical terrains a good story was not so much the issue as was survival. Did you really want to meet an eel-demon by the bridge? Happily you had no choice; the ancient traveler to the river or lake was bound to meet a monster. The lakes, river ways, and the coastal islands were places for a teeming variety of demons and sprites from all religions. Naturally, they tended to be women. According to the cosmic polarities of yin and yang, water produced the female demon or the goddess. Spirits of fertility and of eroticism gathered as well in the mists; and the tales of waterside visits tended to be poignant and ominous.

The Yangtze River, which bisects China at midline like a belt, is the first among these legend-rich waterways. The shrines, temples, and attendant stories that punctuate the shoreline are impossible to count. The most famous site along the Yangtze River is a spectacular chain of narrows called the Three Gorges; it channels and churns the river halfway along its course.

A great complex of legends adheres to the cliffs of the Three Gorges. One of the peaks towering above the river has been known for at least two thousand years as Shamaness Mountain. On its cliffs and ledges, among the wild growth of rain-soaked green, the people of the ancient feudal state of Chu practiced shamanism. The shaman priests and priestesses performed rainmaking and fertility magic, as well as healing arts and spiritual journeys. At the core of the ceremony the shaman or priest-king met the Divine Woman (Shen Nü), or the shamaness met the River

God. The divine meeting was, in fact, a divine mating; high up in the storm and rain, at the mountain's height, the union of mortal and goddess made the land fertile.

Of course, some disapproved of all the fun. The great feudal states to the north, long dedicated to the sober rituals of Confucianism, looked aghast at the Chu magic: "They believe in the power of shamanesses and spirits," harrumphed one northern observer, "and are much addicted to lewd religious rites."[3] The "lewdness" the northerner noted was not entirely in the eye of the beholder. Chu magic involved a sexual encounter that left little to the imagination. In Chu rites men and women sang seductive songs to accompany provocative dances. This, to the North, was unacceptable. From the ancient through the medieval periods we read of magistrates—the Northern culture police—eradicating shrines and banning rituals.

Despite such oppression, however, the legends continued, but in altered forms. The poet Qu Yuan mimicked the shamanic drama of the doomed encounter to lament his political fate; his epic poetry repeats the shaman's narrative. Daoists recast the tales of the water goddesses in prayers and hymns; the shamanic goddess of rain became a Daoist goddess. Even into modern times the goddess comes up for air. From the tales of lake Dongting from the eighteenth century, to films of riverside encounters, all have a man searching for the goddess of the lake. Though shamanism became the outcast religion in China, banned by law, the story of the river goddess remained. "The quest of the goddess"—so termed by David Hawkes—has been recast in poems and tales for two thousand years.

Following the flow of the Yangtze River, we will come eventually to the network of rivers, lakes, and canals that make up the Yangtze Delta, one of the ancient sites of Chinese civilization. On this riverine land-scape villagers early on produced rice and developed trade. This lush land also generated some of the richest layering of legends. When the folklorist, Wolfram Eberhard, traveled the river ways of Southern China in the 1930's he remarked that every bend in the river seemed to have a shrine to a local goddess.[5]

White Snake is first among the Yangtze Delta legends. She is a gorgeous shape shifter who seduced and married a hapless merchant and, for a time, thwarted all priestly attempts to subdue her. She is, of course, a snake shape shifter, but she is a feminine monster of extreme contradictions: both a snake-creature and woman, both romanticized and demonized. She assumes the roles of healer, warrior, wife, magician, comic and thief, and ends her life as a chastised demon, crushed beneath a pagoda by a devout but dull priest.

But despite her heterodox identity and final punishment, White Snake is a kind of unofficial tutelary god of the watery urban South, emblematic of its energy and charisma. She is resolutely allied with the sites in and around the Southern city of Hangzhou; she coiled herself up by a famous Hangzhou bridge, slithered out of a famous Hangzhou lake, was a busy merchant's wife among all the bustle of this prosperous Song Dynasty city, and was finally tamed when a Hangzhou priest squashed her under the famous Leifeng Pagoda of Hangzhou.

And as a Hangzhou citizen, she is its most famous legend. Her cultural weight is a force to reckon with. She is deeply popular. There is hardly a medium that has not portrayed her. Her tale has replicated infinitely; from oral performances in village halls, in woodblock prints, and then in opera, on to cartoons, television and film, she is a cottage industry for every venue of storytelling.

Perhaps we may look back to the lands of Hangzhou for a reason. It may be that those "lewd" southerners were still charmed by watery, powerful women, still loved the woman of Shamaness Mountain who was fertile and dangerous. As the city Hangzhou expanded in wealth and influence, her popular arts and popular heroes likewise gained influence. The South, through the permutations and infinite retellings of

the legend acquired an urban anti-hero. White Snake became a kind of mercurial heroine of the bumptious South, a primitive eel demon of the lakeside, changed by generations of storytellers into an urbane, charming and tragic eel demon of the lakeside.

One of the most frightening places in the Southern landscape is the abandoned place; for, if a river trip is disastrous, a walk past an abandoned courtyard could set your moral compass adrift and bring you deep unease. Ruined towns, neglected cemeteries, long silenced temples, weed filled compounds, foggy pathways at night and even the quieted back garden are half-landscapes, places of failed cultivation being reclaimed by the supernatural; and these territories yield the most eerie encounters. Hangzhou and West Lake, as well as the temples dotting the surrounding hills, have many ghost stories, and Suzhou, with its web of canals and once magnificent gardens, hosts these tales as well.

Gardens gave rise to a malign cast; female demons—the fox fairy, suicide ghost, or unsettled spirit—are common occupants. These women are the sexual predators of Chinese legend, eager to collect some "manly energies" from the always innocent male. A lonely young man at his desk in the night is an open invitation to a female demon; lurking in the garden is required, which is very convenient for the storyteller. A few stray weeds, and a sexual encounter is imminent.

In the play *Mistress and Maid* we hear the voice of one of these demons translated by Cyril Birch.

But first, the setting:

> Silent, empty the green clad steps
> Chirping of crickets all about
> No sooner sinks the evening sun
> Than misty moon begins to rise.
> Will-o-the wisps, green glow of lamp
> Flickering as curtain quivers.[6]

A misty moonrise and flickering lamp surely spell trouble; a ghost or shape shifter is just waiting for her entrance. Only the most naïve young scholar lingers long in such landscapes. And sure enough, there she is, the observing, predatory woman, obsessed with the man she watches.

The ghost speaks:

> Now in this eerie shimmering
> Between the twilight and the moon glow
> Softly I pass the trellised roses
> To where a flickering lantern,
> Its candle dripping waxen tears,
> Is sole companion to a handsome, sad, young scholar.
> He stirs my heart till I can't resist—
> Can't resist this longing,
> A demon fever this time,
> Stronger than ever in my mortal life.[7]

Southern storytellers had an easy cue for this sort of tale. Like the watery spot for Big Grandpa's eel demon, this garden had a ghost well prepared for her entrance. Of course, this ghost is a more ambiguous demon than Big Grandpa's, but the subtlety in her portrayal does not undermine her attachment to place. Her half human nature, her spying in from the dark, and her "demon fever" all belong in this lush night time garden, as quiet as the eel demon's bridge.

Despite the malign presence of demon lovers, however, other, more benign, goddesses reigned in the South. One of the great goddesses of China has a Southern address. The island of Putuoshan lies off the coast of central China, not far from where the Yangtze empties into the sea. This island was again an ancient site dedicated to local worship of a goddess to protect mariners. With the advent of great merchant clans and shipping industry, as Buddhism became more popular in China, the Buddhist Goddess Guan Yin assumed the duties. On the island of Putuoshan she watches now for mariners, and the goddess—who was actually a male deity in India—became fully transformed into a goddess of mercy.

But if Southern waters summoned up goddesses and female shape shifters, the waters of the North called up the masculine world. The Yellow River, considered the cradle of Chinese civilization, flows through northern China, racing down off the Tibetan plateau and bending eastward in a giant "S" curve. Beijing in the far Northeast was the capital of China since the 1400's. The great royal compound called the Forbidden City holds the myths allied with the Son of Heaven of the Ming and Qing dynasties. As Son of Heaven, the Emperor was both ruler and deity, and his power and his corruption made for great legends.

In the Northwest the Yellow River and its tributary, the Wei River, flow near the capitals of ancient dynasties and feudal states: Chang'an

and Loyang lie next to these Northern rivers. In these ancient centers the founding myths of the early Empire arose: the sage kings and culture heroes, the river tamers and creators of civilization. The official Imperial cult practiced in these cities was rigidly tied to land and season, as the Emperor's actions echoed heavenly change; he greeted seasonal change in rituals of the land.

But this region of China was not hermetically sealed. Despite being the locus of the mythology of empire, the cities of the Northwest turned their eyes to the far west, beyond the ancient and medieval borders. It has been naively asserted that China was insular, that she rarely traded beyond her borders, that she was incurious about foreign peoples and customs. This is nonsense. Chang'an, especially in Medieval times, had a great curiosity for the exotic. Thousands of tales of strange encounters came from this point where the silk route begins. Chinese collections of legends, not to mention the great historical compendia, are filled with foreign lore and foreign knowledge tied to land. Foreign monks brought the texts and divine talismans or cures from India or from silk route cities, and Chinese pilgrims brought back knowledge from Tashkent, Samarkand or Persia. Shrines in Loyang, Chang'an and points west along the trade route mark the legends of these places.

Mountains

The Daoist Master Ge Hong warned: "All mountains whether large or small, contain gods and powers, and the strength of these divinities is directly proportional to the size of the mountains." Then he added cheerily, "Mountains are not to be entered lightly." But Ge Hong—a traveler of the fourth century—was simply being practical. A mountain journey in the mystified landscape of the past–and of the tale—was no less risky than a boat ride.

Ancient beliefs had a ready stock of surprises in store for the hiker. Deities, demons, miraculous events, not to mention strange gifts from the supernatural world—swords, talismans and secret texts—readily appeared to the mountain traveler. Buddhists encountered the divine on Mount Emei, Daoists on Mount Mao. Even the ordinary pilgrim could run into magic on one of the Five Sacred Mountains. Indeed, mountains were themselves divine; they were gods who attracted the devout; and tales of mountain encounters are ancient and resonant.

First among the pilgrim tale is the tale of the Emperor. On his pilgrimage to Mount Tai (*Taishan*), with a royal retinue, he traveled the treacherous heights laden with imperial gifts, paying homage to the Lord of Mount Tai, or rather the Lord who is Mount Tai. But this Imperial trip was hardly a holiday. It was an ordeal; a misstep had consequences. Mountain gods could be very unforgiving; the pilgrim-Emperor was tried by his journey. A successful visit was a sign of heavenly favor: the mandate was secure. Storms, however, were ominous. Inclement weather on the Sacred Mountain was not a matter of inconvenience; it was proof of the God-Mountain's disapproval, of his withdrawing the mandate. A mountain downpour proved, in much too public a fashion, that the current reign was flawed.

But the Emperor was simply another pilgrim. Mountain stories all had the bite of retribution in them. Divine encounters with angry gods—of any denomination—were possible. On Mount Tai the Judge of Souls, The Jade Emperor, ruled the world of the dead; an encounter with him could be very worrisome.

But if Emperors could be chastened, Daoists could be enlightened. For Daoist storytellers the mountain itself had lessons to teach. Of course, many stories tell of divine sightings; the great cast of male and female deities made frequent appearances to the devout high on the dangerous paths. Strange beings with sacred talismans or documents might change a traveler's life, and the mystic—male or female—might appear and reveal the secrets of longevity.

But the stories of the mountain journey were not confined to the tales of a divine encounter; for Daoists, the mountain journey itself was transformative. Escaping the mundane, shedding categories, reaching the path and abandoning the herd, the mountain journey gave the gift of singularity. The mountain story had a twist of revelation in it.

In the tale of one mountain encounter, the famous poet Ruan Ji stalks a great mountain mystic hoping to explore with him the recondite esoterica of the cosmos. The poet is himself a famous iconoclast, infamous, in fact, for his drunken defiance of convention. But even he has a lesson to learn about the mountain.

In *A New Account of Tales of the World* the poet, Ruan Ji, seeks out the Great Mystic of Sumen Mountain. Journeying for days, he finally finds him perched on the edge of a steep cliff high up in the peaks. Ruan Ji asks the great man about the Dao, but is met only with silence. Apparently sure of his own knowledge, and hoping for further enlightenment, the poet opens the study session with his own contributions, discoursing on "The Way of the Arcane Quietude." And when he is met only with silence, he continues with a solemn discussion of the "Excellence of Ultimate Virtue." But the great mystic is deeply uninterested and with studied calm, simply looks off into the clouds.

Ruan Ji, after hours of this, finally manages to take the hint. He gets up and turns away heading down the mountain, whistling to himself absently. But, at the sound of the whistle, the strange man turns suddenly and says with a laugh, "Do it again." Ruan Ji gives out a second whistle as he heads on down the path. After a bit, when the poet is halfway down the ridge, he hears an amazing noise. Turning to look up the cliff, he sees that "the Strange Mystic is whistling away, creating astonishing airs, like the sound of an orchestra of wind instruments."[8]

In short order, Ruan Ji has been given a typical Daoist lesson—a mountain lesson—on what mountains offer. He learns from the mystic of the cliffs—not the conventions of dogma explained at length—but the defiance of dogma. He receives the Daoist meta-lesson in "free and easy wandering," learning that wordlessness is the authentic expression, that non-purposive action is liberating and that intellectual showoffs are annoying and tedious.

The Traveler and the Storyteller

In China the mythology of travel is part of the narrative of magic, for travel converts—at least for the duration of the journey—the ordinary into the extraordinary. Any traveler is suddenly a pilgrim, which is great news for the storyteller, as Big Grandpa certainly knew. Even long familiar pathways will have some twists; the landscape in China has the means to surprise.

The 17th century writer Yuan Hongdao loved the journey. He wrote about his mountain hikes, and he was always thrilled by the potential of the mountain, for if he did not discover enchanted beings, he did discover his own enchanted state. The journey restored his mind to a sense of wonder.

On his trip to Mount Hua, Yuan described his passion for the mountain hike.

> At Shansun pavilion, I put on my turban:
> I'm a pilgrim of the clouds—
> off to pay my respects to the rocky crags.
> The waters have their secret arts for flowing beyond this
>   world.
> The mountains are a drug that lightens the body.[9]

Yuan assumes the turban and staff as an avowed pilgrim, out to find the universe beyond the gates. Invoking the adepts of the past, he performs a ritual obeisance and finds, in the waters, "secret arts." Mountain travel is, for him, the alchemist's decoction—"a drug that lightens the body."

And if he plays the adept in this poem, he plays the devout Emperor in an essay. Climbing Flew-Here Peak near Hangzhou, Yuan Hongdao mimics the Royal Pilgrim on Mount Tai. As if sent by ancestral dicta to worship the spirit of the place, Yuan discovers a mountain that is animated, like the surface of a shaman's map.

> Of all the mountains around West Lake, Flew-Here Peak must be considered the best. One could not do justice to its angry posture, even by calling it a thirsty tiger or a galloping lion. One could not do justice to its strange form, even by speaking of gods weeping and demons rising. Nor could one do justice to its twisting, turning transformations, even by comparing it with the calligraphy of Crazy Chang or the painting of Wu Tao-tzu....

The angry posture of the hill, the demonic look of its form and calligraphic shapes all evoke the Lord who is Mount Tai; these mountains are organic, animate and active.

Finally, Yuan makes the summit. "Altogether I have climbed Flew-Here Peak five times. The first time I made the trip with Huang Taoyuan.... we wore unlined shirts rolled up in back, and we made it right to the summit." But what interests interests this pilgrim is not the summit, but the rocks that speak to him on the way up, for he finds in the trip a full sense of the strangeness of the journey. The hike along the surface of the ominous place restores his innocence. He shouts out with a childlike thrill.

"Each time we came upon an unusual rock," he said," we would, without fail, go wild with delight and let out loud shouts."[10]

Yuan's shouts of pleasure are like his traveler's staff and turban;

they announce the pilgrim's humility and his ready sense of astonishment. He anticipates the strange, lest he bypass the magic of the spot, for in Chinese folklore, travel is sport for the attuned, not for the dull, not for the jaded. The role of the traveler is to play the naïf; cynics should stay home.

Likewise storytellers know that strange encounters happen on strange roads; and so they assume the role of traveler. They begin the tale the way a shaman's handbook begins: with a journey. On the look-out for magic, travelers are magnets for the monstrous. Storytellers in the West open the tale with "Once upon a time…," as time is mystified and made eerie. But Chinese storytellers invoke the strange by reordering space, by mystifying that landscape long established as ready to shift.

Are we surprised, then, that Mo Yan tells us that his Big Grandpa was a country doctor who "often saw his patients in the middle of the night." In other words, Big Grandpa was a traveler. Not the sedentary homebody, he was out and about at all hours, on the road when the rest of the village slept, the honorary stranger in suddenly strange landscapes.

But house calls make great material. At every turn in the road, every landmark or rise, a god or demon, messenger or magician, could appear at the roadside with some small request for assistance, and he could run into the kind of trouble we love to hear about.

Notes to the Introduction:

1   Yuan Zhongdao, "Shou dajie wushi, xu," in Yuan Zhongdao, *Kexue zhai wenji*, (Shanghai: Beiye shanfang, 1936) p. 12.

2   Mo Yan, "My Three American Books" Howard Goldblatt, trans., *World Literature Today*, vol. 74, 33 Summer 2000.

3   Richard Strassberg, *The Chinese Bestiary: Strange Creatures from the "Guideways Through Mountains and Seas."* Berkeley: The University of California Press, 2002, pp 126-127.

4   David Hawkes, *The Songs of the South, An Anthology of Ancient Chinese Poems by Qu Yuan and Other Poets*, New York, Penguin, 1985, p. 18.

5   Wolfram Eberhard, "On the Folklore of Chekiang," in *Studies in Chinese Folklore*, Indiana University Folklore Institute Monograph Series, vol. 23, Bloomington, 1970, p. 31.

6   Meng Chengshun, *Mistress and Maid, (Jiao Hongji)* Cyril Birch, translator and editor, New York, Columbia University Press, 2001, p. 268.

7   Ibid., p. 255.

8   Richard Mather, trans. *A New Account of Tales of the World by Liu I-ch'ing with Commentary by Liu Chun*, Minneapolis, University of Minnesota Press, 1976, p. 331.

9   Yuan Hongdao, *Pilgrim of the Clouds, Poems and Essays from Ming China*, trans. Jonathan Chaves, New York and Tokyo, Weatherhill, 1978, p. 59.

10 Ibid., p. 99.

PART 1

The North

The Storyteller

Liu Jingting was pockmarked and dark of complexion. He was a great storyteller. For one episode of an epic he could charge one silver tael, and you had to send a letter of reservation and make a deposit ten days in advance. Before he began his performance, he demanded the absolute full attention of the audience. No one moved or seemed to breathe. And if he caught sight of a servant whispering or stretching he would remain silent. When he performed, he could dig down into the minutest details of a scene, or sound out like a huge bronze bell. At the turning point of a tale, he would shout and yell in a voice loud enough to shake the house. Even after all evening of storytelling, at midnight, he would just dust the table before him, trim the lamp wick down, drink some tea from his porcelain cup, and then continue along in a mellow tone to unfold his tale.

Zhang Dai (1597-1684)

Xi'an and the Route West

Guan Yin

His Royal Highness—the Illustrious Theocrat, Emperor of the Great Tang Dynasty, receiver of tribute from the far reaches of Inner Asia, commander of armies far to the South, even to Vietnam, known to posterity as The Cultured Ancestor—was exceedingly fond of clams. On his throne in the Capital City of Chang'an he ordered clams for three of his five meals, each and every day. During the ninth course, between the second soup and the fourth seafood, the Imperial Chef of the Imperial Clam prepared an elegant, fresh, succulent platter.

Now, as you know, the capital of the Tang Dynasty was Chang'an, a great city in the west of China, a city that turned its face to the empires of Inner Asia, so it was no easy matter to bring clams to the Emperor, the Illustrious Theocrat. It was only through the bitter labors of thousands that he ate such a delicacy. Every day in the dim light before dawn, clams would be gathered by the ocean fishermen of Zhejiang and then packed by porters in cold seaweed, wet sand and ice, then rapidly loaded on relay mounts that sped the Imperial highway.

The Royal Couriers on their powerful mounts rushed headlong toward the capital. They scattered all travelers before them, their banners announcing the Imperial mission. Changing mounts in the walled towns, they rattled up the streets and back out the city gates, racing north-north-west through three provinces, all the way out to the dry landscape of Chang'an. In three days the clams had to arrive fresh and still living, because the Emperor's whim is the world's command and the Emperor does not eat spoiled food.

But though the Emperor gathered the riches of Asia and had a stronghold that surpassed the treasuries of Rome and of Baghdad, yet he never

paid a bill. The fishermen, the dock-workers, the stable grooms and the riders and even the cooks gave their labors just because the Imperial Command so decreed.

One day on a fine summer evening, the Imperial Shipment of Fresh Clams failed to arrive. The Illustrious Theocrat would be in want of his daily course of clams. The Royal Attendant of the Supply Docks notified the Master of Fish and Ocean Creatures, who then reported hastily to the Governors of Kitchens, who subsequently relayed it in writing to the Chief Chef of the Imperial Supper, who took this aforesaid document directly to the Master Cook—who saw it and immediately collapsed. The kitchen staff gathered together in mute shock, none daring to take a full breath.

Finally, timorously, the Royal Chef of the Imperial Clam made a suggestion. "Actually," he said in a tiny voice, "we do have one clam that remains from our previous shipment. It is still very alive and smells as fresh as if it just came from the ocean, and it is very grand in size."

By now, the Imperial Repast had proceeded apace, and the fourth seafood, after the second grain, before the tenth course following the palate cleansing soup had been served, and the Royal Clam Server was waiting. So, hurrying to the hot stove, the staff steamed up the giant clam in fine herbs and wine, surrounded it in spring onions and brought it out to the Imperial table. The Emperor seemed exceptionally pleased. The clam was enormous—twenty times the usual shell,—surely an Imperial clam meant for the Imperial Palate. The Royal Personage could only imagine the fine flavors the meat would yield—he sat eagerly with a happy expression on his Royal Visage, licking the Imperial Saliva that the delightful aroma produced. As the Clam Shell Opener stepped up to pry the shell apart, however, he found the shell sealed like iron; all the

prying, poking, straining and yanking had no effect. The clam was as tight as a rock crevice on the slope of Mount Tai.

The Emperor frowned.

But all of a sudden, as if by signal, the clam began to open. With a steady fluid motion, as if on divine hinges, the top shell reared open to expose the shiny silver and chalky white shell walls. The Emperor peered down inside. He gasped at what he saw. There, standing inside, was a finely detailed, miniature, astonishingly sweet statue of the Goddess of Mercy, the Bodhisattva Guan Yin, exquisitely carved. But the Emperor was most surprised by her lovely expression. It was mild and soft, as if she forgave all the sins in the world.

The Emperor was greatly abashed by such a sight, for he knew immediately—in his heart of hearts—that the Buddhist Goddess—who hears even the smallest call for mercy from even the tiniest voice in the empire—had taken pity on the boat men, the fisher folk, the portage men and relay riders, even the royal cooks—all who served without fail and without complaint his royal taste and royal whim.

So the Emperor decreed throughout the Empire that all would know the mercy of Guan Yin and all would know her divine authority. He commanded that carved statues of Guan Yin—carved just like the fine miniature he had found in the shell—be placed in Buddhist temples throughout the empire: throughout both the North and the South. And, in honor of the fisher folk of Zhejiang, he called her "The Goddess Guan Yin of the Southern Sea," so that, like all great goddesses of the sea, she would watch over mankind in times of fear and danger.

And he decreed as well, to the Royal Kitchen, who informed the royal Attendant of Fish and Ocean Creatures, who relayed it dutifully to the Imperial Relay Stations, who thence reported it on to the Imperial Boatmen, and, finally, to the Emperor's own Clam Gatherers, that the Emperor, the Illustrious Theocrat, would only require clams once a week.

The Golden Millet Dream

Once upon a time when the great Tang armies had quelled the barbarians, and all points of the compass were at peace, there was a young scholar named Lü Dongbin. Now, Lü's destiny was to become a great Daoist Immortal; but when he first arrived in the capital of Chang'an, the center of Imperial power, all he knew were his ambitions. Indeed, like many a young man of fine family, Lü had his heart set on success in the Court Examination. He dreamed that, with a brilliant score, he could achieve rank in the Imperial Bureaucracy, and become a magistrate or even a high court official. So with his hopes set high, and his knapsack stuffed with his books and his scholar's robe, Lü arrived in Chang'an and found a fine inn to stay at not far from the massive gates of the city he had just entered.

The courtyard of the inn was newly swept and, as he entered the hall, the bright fire took the chill off his long journey in the snow. Lü shook the cold off as he came into the little hall, setting his knapsack down by the table set for the travelers. As he eased into his seat, the innkeeper promised him a fine supper made from the specialties of his northern kitchen: some venison, a little rabbit and mutton, and, of course, some special golden millet. Hungry from his journey he turned to watch the innkeeper at the stove as he set the millet to boil, knowing that he had not long to wait. In the meantime, he noticed the odd appearance of his fellow traveler—an old and rather eccentric sort of man, who called himself Zhongli Quan. Now Zhongli Quan was no ordinary traveler, but

a Daoist immortal. And when this immortal saw this fine, intelligent, forthright young scholar, he struck up a conversation. "I see, Sir, that you are here to study for the great Imperial Exams: that you have dedicated your life to the noble goal of serving the Emperor and the Ancestors."

"Indeed, sir," replied Lü Dongbin. "It is true. I hope to find my fortune here in the Capital. Perhaps, Revered Master, you could give me some advice on what I am to do?"

"But what can I, a humble wayfarer, do for such a fine scholar, as yourself," protested the old man.

"But you appear to be a sage," declared Lü, "and, surely, you know secrets that may serve me well in the Great Examination before me.

"Perhaps you are right," the old man conceded. "Here. Take this pillow and have a rest. Let me think how I may be of service to you, in this, 'the Great Examination,' as you have called it."

Lü Dongbin lay his head down and with a deep sigh felt the fatigue of the journey begin to ease. As he rested on the hard porcelain pillow he noticed an opening at the end. A man stood in the lip as if by a gate and beckoned him inside. The hole grew larger, and Lü stood up and walked in with ease. The man took him back out of the inn, along through the Chang'an streets—now bathed in Spring sunlight—past the crowds in the market place, down the great avenue that ran northward to the Palace, arriving finally at the palace wall in the center of the great city. There he found throngs of men staring at the examination scores that had been posted on the palace wall. He saw several scholars from his own district and there before him was his own name written near the top. He felt an immense surge of relief, for he knew now that he could return home with honor.

Because of his achievement in the Examination, Lü was awarded rank and position: he became Collator in the Imperial Library, and a member of the Hanlin Academy where his scholarship and skill in debate marked him as a Worthy of the Realm. With such success, he was soon transferred to serve as Magistrate in Shanxi province, where he was known as a meticulous magistrate, with a reputation for both filial conduct and useful proclamations. After five years in service, he received a promotion to the capital. In Chang'an he took office within the Court, as the "Diarist of Standing and Repose." He stood at the Emperor's side and became a valued counselor in matters of Imperial debate. Soon after, he became Attendant Supervisor of the Department of State Affairs, the officer who drafted legislation.

He had by this time been married for ten years. His wife came originally from his home district, from a wealthy clan. She was of exceptional beauty and piety. She established with him a fine estate in the capital that became renown for their brilliant carriages and fine retinue, as well as their grand receptions and entertainments. Within a few years she had given birth to four sons. Lü's dignity increased and his reputation grew day by day.

After some years in court, the empire suffered a terrible crisis: the rebellion of An Lushan tore the empire apart and the land north of the Yellow River was overrun by the Tibetan forces. They attacked both Shazhou and Guazhou prefectures and killed the local governors. The Emperor appointed Lü Dongbin to serve as Governor of the Northern Circuit and Regional Commander of the armies of the North. Lü routed the Tibetan forces, cut off seven thousand heads, and brought peace to the Sub-Celestial Realm. When he built fortifications to pacify the region, altars were erected in his honor.

Before long however, the Prime Minister became envious of Lü's successes and stirred up trouble against him. Officials at court slandered him and claimed he was in league with the border peoples. Stirred by their warnings, the Emperor decreed Lü was to be arrested and executed for treason. When the officers arrived at his gate, he said to his wife, "In my native town in Shandong, my family has a farm with twenty acres, enough to support us in our old age. What possessed me to seek an official's salary? If only I could put off these robes and take us back in our family cart." He drew his knife and was about to slit his throat when his wife prevented him.

The execution order was soon commuted, however, as the conspirators fell out and their leader died; so Lü's punishment was commuted from death to banishment. After some years, when Lü's son's were all grown, the Emperor learned that the charges were false and so Lü was brought back to serve in the Imperial City. He became Grandee Extraordinary in the Department of the Secretariat and was awarded a feudal title. Lü's sons achieved fine positions as well. His sons, Quan, Wei and Di, served as Magistrates and his youngest son, Yi, became Vice Director in the Department of State Affairs at the young age of twenty-eight.

Finally, after years of service, Lü became ill and weary with age and worry. So he petitioned the Emperor to relieve him of his duties that he might return back to his childhood home. Lü humbly addressed the Emperor:

"Your servant came as a humble student from Shandong; yet he has, despite his lack of talent, encountered the Divine Munificence of his Royal Majesty. For fifty years since my first post I have, despite my base and ignorant manner, been graced with rewards. On leaving the capital the banners due the Imperial Representative gathered in my train. When I returned I was raised up to be Prime Minister. In managing the matters

31

of the Court, I find now that many years have passed; diligent to attend to court manners, I find that old age has taken me by surprise. This year I will be eighty and find I am too ravaged by weakness to serve longer. I submit this humble petition that I may take leave of your Pious Presence."

The Emperor himself composed the reply:

"You have served me loyally for these years and now in your illness I have sent the royal physician to look after you. Please take extra care that we may see you again attending to us in Court."

That night Lü died.

Still deep within the memories of his life, Lü sat up. Looking around he seemed to feel the weariness of his eighty years, and yet there by his side was the knapsack he had carried in; and there was the old man still at the table, now packing the pillow into his bag. Yet Lü could clearly recall his time in Court, his wife and his sons and his plans and challenges, the battles with the barbarians and the endless tasks in the government posts. But here, suddenly, in the evening light, under the eaves of the welcoming inn, he saw the light play across the floor, and heard the bustling sounds of Chang'an coming to him beyond the courtyard.

Suddenly Lü Dongbin knew. He knew that all those years he had passed as a fine official had, indeed, all taken place; but he also knew that all his cares and all his fears—all the fury at the betrayals—had simply occurred in that whisper of time he lay on the pillow. The years of life—with his constant desire to serve and succeed—had tumbled by in that rustle of minutes the innkeeper had taken as he stood by the stove, stirring the pot, as the golden millet, promised for supper, came to the boil.

White Horse

White Horse felt the wind change as the dawn light broke over the sand horizon. Shuddering with the approach of the storm, she flattened her ears and pawed the ground. Looking down at Kumarajiva as he packed up the campsite, she shoved his shoulder with her muzzle. Recognizing her signs as if they were human speech, the sacred traveler knew their time was short. They had to seek protection in the ruined city ahead or be caught in the whirlwind. As the sands rolled in from the west, the horse and rider struggled for three hours, until, finally, they tucked in behind the broken walls. There they settled down for some meager rations and waited out the terrible winds and roiling sands for two days.

Their journey together had lasted ten years. Kumarajiva had left the great estate of his family in Kashmir, India, determined to travel the silk route to China. He knew his mission was bold: the great Han Dynasty had fallen, and the land of China was in disarray. But he was determined to bring the word of the Buddha along a journey of six thousand miles: through Parthia and Khotan and Kashgar, along the Gansu Corridor, and on to the cities of Loyang and Chang'an. But no journey was too long for Kumarajiva; for he longed to bring to China the scriptures, the prayers, the tales of the Buddha, as well as the true accounts of the Bodhisattva of Salvation, called Guan Yin; for Guan Yin—in her feminine incarnation—has compassion for mankind, gives solace to the suffering, and protects mothers and their babes.

So, parting with his family, mounted on White Horse, he set out when he was 30 years old; and with her intelligence he had survived. She had found hidden springs in the Taklamakan Desert and had struck out with

33

her powerful hooves when the mountain assassins rushed him from the cliffs. She had sprung forward like a lion to defend him from predators and now, as they reached the edge of China, she had stretched out her great thick neck and sniffed the danger of the whirlwind. So Kumarajiva knew he sat on a Buddha-Horse, a divine horse, a horse who carried him just as Guan Yin carries man on her Bark of Salvation.

After ten years Kumarajiva and White Horse came finally to the town of Dunhuang, on the easternmost edge of the Taklamakan Desert at the borders of China. He saw in the distance the great Mogao caves filled with sculptures made by the devout; they loomed majestically out of the yellow sand. Beyond the caves he knew the Gansu Corridor awaited, then the sacred caves of Maijishan, and finally the city of Chang'an. He knew his journey was coming near to completion.

Now, Kumarajiva had heard of the great caves and longed to see their massive sculptures, rising hundreds of feet into the sky, carved by pilgrims to display their faith; but he was so footsore from his travels and so parched from the dust that he stopped at an inn to rest for the night. As he stopped at the well to drink he caught his reflection: "How grey I have become," he said to himself. Then he looked at his Buddha-Horse and saw that her once grey neck and dark muzzle were now a brilliant white. Kumarajiva handed the reins to a servant of the inn. "Take her to the stable, I will check on her later," he said quietly. He reached up to the fine neck and elegant crest and gave a firm stroke, leaned his head to her shoulder, and spoke a prayer to the Goddess Guan Yin. White horse dropped her head and acknowledged him. Then, with a weary look to the inside of the hall, Kumarajiva turned and entered with his pack.

The evening was still, the sunset vivid, and the cool in the air was welcome. He finished his meal and, for the first time in many a year, chanted his sutras with a lightened heart. He spoke his favorite passage in the last paragraph of The Lotus of the Good Law and fell sound asleep. In his sleep, he dreamed that White Horse spoke to him. "Teacher, I am, in fact, the White Dragon of the Western Sea. I was sent to aid you—that the Teachings of the Buddha might arrive safely in China. Now that you have entered the Pass and the road ahead holds no danger, I shall accompany you no further." Kumarajiva heard the words and felt in his dream a desperate grief; he clung to White Horse and pleaded.

With a start, Kumarajiva woke up. The night was almost over and the sun just lighting the earth; quickly he got up and walked through the dawn out to the stable. There he found his horse lying down very still in the straw. Soundlessly in the night, when the town was fast asleep White Horse had grown ill with colic. For hours she had ached, and then quietly had sunk to her knees, lay down on her side and died. Kumarajiva found her there. He had slept through the night, not knowing she had suffered, for though she had pawed the ground in her troubles, she had made neither moan nor whisper; for beasts, when they suffer, do not weep.

Silently he knelt beside her. He stroked her massive white flank and cried. Then he had her buried there, in the yard of the inn, in the place that became the White Horse Dagoba. It still stands today.

For twenty-nine years Kumarajiva remained in China, translating and teaching, until he died in 413. He lectured on the Law of the Buddha, interpreted the words of the Buddha and founded a great translation center where the sutras were taught. But his most famous work was his translation of the Lotus of the Good Law, wherein it is said that the Bodhisattva, who stayed among men to lead them to the Truth, comes to man as the Goddess Guan Yin. In this sacred guise, she protects babes and sailors and travelers, and horses and all beasts, indeed, all who

ask—even without knowing—for her help. For it is said that the Goddess Guan Yin commands the Bark of Salvation, and she will take us, if we ask her, just like White Horse, on our journeys.

Fan Yuqi and the First Emperor

At the end of the Warring States, in the time before China was unified, there was a great clan—the Fan family—that lived in the state of Qin. The men of the Fan lineage were all brilliant generals. For generations past, the grandfathers and the fathers—and now the sons and sons again—had led the Qin armies to hundreds of victories in decades of feudal service to the kings of the Qin State.

But in 247 B.C a new Prince of Qin became the king. The new king used the Fan clan to carry out his plan of world conquest. He sent off the Fan generals in his endless wars. They led his armies; 10,000 strong marched on Qi and 20,000 marched on Chu; they fought too in the military campaigns northward to Korea and southward to Vietnam, and they helped implement his harsh laws, so that the machine of conquest was made efficient.

Through all his conquests the Fan clan served the king loyally, as their ancestors had served the Qin rulers before him. But they served him in fear, for they all knew that serving the king of Qin was like tending the dragon in his lair: take care lest you stroke the scales backward. And sure enough, as the king of Qin increased his power, he grew fearful; and he came to mistrust the power of the great Fan clan. He feared that their loyal battalions, their skills as generals, and their dignity as a great clan would be used against him, so he imprisoned the grand father and the father, confiscated the clan's properties and their walled cities, seized the women of the family to serve as entertainers in the palace, and pursued and captured every male child of the clan to exterminate the line.

Fan Yuqi, the youngest son of the clan, escaped. On the eve of a great battle when he had summoned his troops to fight for Qin, he fled the kingdom in the dead of night. He abandoned his feudal estates and his ancestral fields and crept like a beggar into hiding. For one year he skulked from back alleys into the wild forests, without shelter or friendship, for no house would take him in, no town-elder receive him. Even the wild tribes to the west of Qin—the Xiongnu herdsman—all refused, for the First Emperor had offered a reward. For bringing the head of Fan Yuqi, the king offered a thousand catties of gold, and a city of ten thousand households.

But one man dared befriend Fan Yuqi, Prince Dan of the tiny state of Yan. The Prince of the royal clan despised the king of Qin; he ached to avenge the cruelty of his rule, he longed to defy his arrogance and power. So he took in the renegade general; and Fan Yuqi was honored in Yan. Now Yan was but a small state, not armed and populous like Qi, nor huge and distant like Chu—but a state rich in iron ore. So all knew that soon the state of Yan would be gone—swallowed whole for its minerals. It only hung on the whim of the Qin king to execute the attack. But Prince Dan of Yan welcomed his dangerous guest and protected him nonetheless.

"This is raw meat before a tiger's paw," said the Prime Minister to Prince Dan of Yan. "You goad the Prince of Qin by welcoming his enemy, and then you hope for some escape. This is madness!"

Then the Court Historian advanced, "You are stirring his fury and abetting catastrophe. It's like a goose feather—you drop it into the flame and—poof!!—we are cooked in a flash. Why do you seek our demise by

succoring his next victim?!"

But Prince Dan of Yan was determined, and he refused to heed their counsel. He honored Fan Yuqi and treated him like a worthy minister. He gave him guards to ring his mansion and met with him every day in fellowship.

"At least consult your Master Assassin Jing Ke," said both advisers. "Let him decide the wisdom of your actions. Let him formulate a plan for our survival."

So Prince Dan of Yan called on Jing Ke, the Master Assassin, and asked him what to do.

Jing Ke suggested a plan. "I will meet with Fan Yuqi, the fugitive from Qin, your now distinguished guest; but first you must give me the master map from the archives of Yan that show all the locations of our valuable mines, for the King of Qin needs these maps to make his conquest worth his while."

"But why do you need the maps!?" said the prince in some alarm.

The Master Assassin gave no answer.

Jing Ke, the assassin, then went to visit the fugitive from Qin, General Fan Yuqi. Fan greeted the strategist in his front hall and escorted him to the reception room. He offered Jing Ke the honored place on the mat and Jing Ke accepted with courtly humility. Gathering his robe, he sat at the low table and accepted the heated liquor he was offered. Jing Ke made a deep nod as he took the cup with both hands. He drank the warm liquor and set down the cup. Then he took two objects from his case and set them down before his host. As Fan Yuqi watched, the famous assassin of Yan laid out the large, finely drawn map of the mines of Yan and, beside it, one square box.

Jing Ke then asked a question of his host: "I have long heard that the king of Qin destroyed your clan and confiscated your properties, seized the women of your clan and ended the rites at the ancestral altars. Is that the case?"

"It is so," replied Fan. "For one year now I have lived in hiding like a fearful, whining, tremulous child, cowering in terror before the might of Qin. I, who was raised in battle, and rode to war in every campaign since I first received command, hide here in luxury. I can hear the ancestors call to me from the sacred altars of my burned and broken clan hall. Every day that I awake and breathe—secure here in Yan—is a foul disgrace to the unavenged honor of my clan."

"I am the Master Strategist and Master Assassin of the state of Yan," said Jing Ke. And I am resolved to kill the Qin King. But though I am determined, yet I can give you no assurance that my strategy will succeed. Indeed, my success is in grave doubt, for even the best of my profession cannot approach the King of Qin. It is decreed on pain of death," Jing Ke

continued, "that no one approaches the throne with a weapon—even his soldiers and guards are so forbidden. The law is strict. If I am to get near him, he must trust me and believe that I am his ally."

Fan Yuqi said, "I understand completely."

Then Fan Yuqi, the fugitive, paused for a moment as if to consider a private thought, and took out his own short sword. He seemed lost in his own reflections as he calmly tested the blade. Then Fan Yuqi looked up at Jing Ke, and said: "May my ancestors favor this, The Great Enterprise." With that comment, he drew the blade across his own throat, in one deep, swift, powerful stroke. Fan's head teetered forward, the blood gushing from the wound, and lolled off its shoulders onto the floor before his collapsing form. Jing Ke took the bloodied head that lay on the mat before him, and placed it firmly in the box.

Then Jing Ke rode on to Qin. He passed two days in his journey and came to the gates of the Qin palace: "I have come to see the Emperor from the state of Yan. I bring with me what he most wants: the map of the Yan mines, and the head of Fan Yuqi." The royal guards saw the head of Fan, removed the weapons from the visitor and allowed him to pass through the corridors and chambers, even into the inner sanctum of the king on his throne.

Jing Ke bowed deeply before the throne of the most powerful man in the realm, and offered his two prizes. The king was suspicious, but he leaned over and peered into the box. He looked pleased by the blood soaked face that looked out sightlessly from within, and spoke with a smile to the head: "Ah, General Fan, so you have returned at last to your home-land. Your ancestors will be pleased, finally, to have you back in your native place." Jing Ke then began to unroll the map of Yan to show

him the array of mines; but, sliding his hand into the innermost roll of the manuscript, he pulled out a dagger and lunged at the king of Qin.

"Seize him!! Hold him!!" shouted the king, but the soldiers in the outer hall were afraid, lest they approach the throne with daggers drawn and violate the law. So the king and the assassin circled the column and lunged at each other jabbing and thrusting, each desperate for a strike. "Come now and seize him!!!" shouted the king again, "I exempt you from my law!!!" The guards rushed in and surrounded Jing Ke and killed him, so that at last the King of Qin was saved. The next day, the king had all the guards executed for violating the law forbidding their approaching the throne armed.

When Prince Dan of Yan heard of the failure of his master strategist Jing Ke, he knew that the revenge on him would be swift. He took his family and killed them all and then committed suicide to avoid the fate of the Fan clan. And, indeed, after the little kingdom of Yan was swal-

45

lowed up, so were all the other states, so that in 221 B.C the Qin Kingdom became the Qin Dynasty and the Qin king became the "First Illustrious God-Emperor" ruling all China under his heavy fist.

The Foreign Monk

Long ago, in the Tang Dynasty, the Imperial City was called Chang'an, "Eternal Peace." Now it is called Xi'an, and is a modern, bustling sort of place. But if you look closer, you will find traces of what was once the greatest capital in the world. In that time of China's vast influence, when her armies swept westward to the Caspian Sea, China was filled with signs of her conquest; foreigners came constantly to China bringing both foreign goods and foreign knowledge. In the Imperial capital of the Tang, streets thronged with musicians and dancers of Kucha, as well as princes of Sogdia, Manichean priests and Nestorian holy men; there were devout Muslims and Jewish ambassadors, and thousands of Buddhists from India. But more numerous than any of these priests and performers were the merchants: Persians, Turks and Arabs trekked the Silk Route to Chang'an to bring all the excellent goods of foreign lands to delight the wealthy of Chang'an. There were the great horses of Farghana used for the game of polo, and the camels for transport, even leopards and cheetahs for the Imperial zoo. And there were goods to eat and admire: lotuses, black pepper, sandalwood, nutmeg and, of course, the golden peaches of Samarkand.

Naturally, a good deal of money could be made by a welcoming inn-keeper. Wang Bu was such a man. He was happy to greet his guests— whether foreign or Chinese—to his commodious inn on the edge of the Western Market near the great wall of the city. Whether they sold leather

goods or horses, or bought silk tapestries or tea, whether they were Turkish moneylenders or examination candidates they gathered at Wang Bu's excellent table.

The great sorrow of Wang Bu's life, however, was his daughter. Wang's daughter was lovely, and bright, educated in the books of filial piety, hard working and sweet, but she had a terrible blemish. Suspended from each nostril was a fine filament of flesh over two inches long; and at the end of each of the filaments was a little bulb of rosy flesh. This was not at all attractive. What is more, if anyone touched them they caused the girl excruciating pain. Wang Bu was desperate to find a cure, and he asked every foreign monk and healer—whether from India, Sogdia, Persia or Kucha—for a cure. He knew that even as the Emperor collected the great prescriptions of the emissaries from the Silk Route, that he too could beg them for their knowledge of their difficult cases.

One day an Indian monk who had been to the Palace with his medical books and herbal recipes stopped by the inn and bowed to Wang Bu. "I understand your daughter is suffering from a disease. Let me see her and I will study the case." Wang told his daughter to come out at once, and the monk considered the peculiar formations. Reaching into his leather case and pulling out a series of pouches, he settled on a powder that smelled of camphor. Holding it close to her nose he blew on it and then, without the slightest hesitation, plucked the filaments, bulbs and all.

Wang Bu was thrilled and offered the monk a hundred taels of silver, but the monk declined. " I lead a solitary life dedicated to the Buddha. I have no use for wealth and finery. However, I would like the two polyps, if I might." Without further ado, the monk packed away the two offending bulbs and left the inn without a glance backward. Wang Bu stood admiring the man for his holy act and fine character.

Suddenly, after the monk had been gone a few minutes, a very fine young man galloped up to the inn on a white horse. He knocked at the door and asked whether the Indian monk with the knapsack of cures had been here. Wang told him enthusiastically about the monk's fine work, but the young man seemed only depressed by the events. Finally he said, "I just missed, I'm afraid, and now I will be in trouble."

"What do you mean," said the innkeeper.

"It seems that two of the musicians of the Divine Orchestra, who had been playing for all the Gods, in the Heavenly Palace, ran away. And it was just learned that they had escaped to your daughter's nose. I was sent by the Lord-on–High to get them, and now the monk has captured them first. I know I will be punished for failing his Divine Lord."

With that he turned his horse and disappeared.

Beijing

Assassination

Yang Jinying was only eighteen years old when she decided to kill the Emperor. She conceived her plan in the Eastern Court of the Forbidden City, among the apartments for the royal women, where she served as Imperial Attendant to the women of the Palace. For Jinying, the plan was simple—suicidal, of course—but simple. All it needed was boldness. A ruthless twist with the Imperial silk cord and the Epochal Ancestor would be another piece of Imperial history.

She had been in the Palace for many years, since she was ten. This Emperor brought serving girls in before their first menses, so that the blood of the first period could be used in his Daoist elixirs of immortality. The Emperor would achieve perfection through the strange magic of the Adepts. So, it seemed, no expense was spared. His great Palace—the halls and compounds, the kitchens and storehouses—were dedicated to Daoist rituals. The High Priests orchestrated grandiose ceremonies lasting days. The famous clerics of Daoism flowed in to the Imperial City to sit below the pavilions, stages and halls erected for the feasts. And the goods! Ambergris, pearls and silks were stockpiled in heaps and mounds like bumper harvests of grain; and suspended above all the ceremonies were the rolls of saffron brocade inscribed with the sacred script and talismans written with pots and pots of ink made with pure gold powder. The Emperor—for all his devotions—would surely ascend in broad daylight as a Daoist God.

As if he were god, she thought, an immortal, a divine visitor to the realms of man. No, she mused, more like a sated pig. In the evening, after platters of food, bowls of wine and hours of debauchery he would lie snoring like an ox in the warm sun. She would simply ride the fat ox

for his last sleep, and avenge the thousands of serving girls who were beaten to death in his court, avenge the thousands of girls brought in for his random pleasures, and avenge, as well, her own life measured out in humiliating sexual favors.

Jinying had conceived the plan alone. But, as if they could read her mind, they came to her. Fifteen serving girls found her and made a pact. They would keep watch: see that the apartment of the Consort was clear, warn if the Household Eunuchs of the Imperial Court approached. One sign from her allies and the plan would wait for another night.

As the late fall sunlight dimmed and the corridors grew dark, Jinying walked through the high north-south passage. She passed the high gates that gave entry to the compounds of the Imperial Concubines, and felt a wave of vertigo at the thought of the killing; but a sense of purpose returned to her. It was November 24, 1542; she would kill the Emperor tonight.

The Household Eunuch saw her pass along the corridor. He glanced slyly at the cord that lay in her right hand. He knew it had been taken from some wall hanging, or scroll, or royal linen; and he smiled to himself as she passed. It was sure to be some secret gift to be sent back to her family as a boast. But he ignored the intended theft; perhaps her little transgression would prove useful for him at some point.

Making her way to the north, she came to the apartments of Grand Consort Cao. She knew that the Imperial concubine was away for an hour or two. Looking around her, she entered the outside gate and took the hallway to the east, coming finally before the outer door of the royal apartment. She stepped over the tall threshold and entered the rooms.

Glancing down at the cord, she noticed its sheen. It was red—perhaps for good luck; it felt heavy, thickly woven of triple braid, strong and smooth—definitely up to the task. The death-knot would slide quickly to his throat.

Weaving back through the public rooms, she found her way to the inner bedroom, she stepped in and the three attendants looked at her, their faces stilled of all expression. Without thinking, she glanced up at the Daoist door guardians glaring down from each wall, and touched the little jade figure at her neck—a pig for her birth year—praying briefly that all malign influences would flee her now.

She saw the Emperor spread out on the bed. A girl of twelve was just climbing down from his fat hips, a look of shattered misery on her face. The girl crept away to the window and watched as Jinying approached. In a few long, fast steps Jinying was by the bedside. The silken linens rustled as she climbed up onto the Imperial body. The noose was at her fingertips and she slipped it down over his head past the brow, pulling it smoothly over his eyes, then his nose, then his chin, until it encircled his throat just above his Adams' apple. He stirred sluggishly beneath her, opening his eyes. He squinted, as if puzzling over the face of Jinying.

Jinying rocked back as she pulled hard on the end of the red cord. Shoving at the slip-knot to run it down the braided silk, she let out a harsh cry from her throat. The Emperor's head jerked up and he was awake, his hands flailing at the cord. Jinying wrapped the end of the cord around her hand and pulled still harder. But the red silk noose did not tighten—the fine red cord refused its job. Jinying reached up to her hair and tore out a silver hairpin. She drove the metal down into the Emperor's left eye and he roared out and shouted for help. One of the girls—one of her allies—fled in a panic to alarm the Empress....

"If the Empress and I had not come running in she would have succeeded," said the Eunuch of the Household. He was walking in the Eastern Compound of the Palace with his ally. "The knot was just a simple square knot—not a death knot—otherwise she would have...."

"Sh-h-h-h! Are you mad even to say such a possibility?! You can be killed for thinking that," said his colleague.

All fifteen of the girls were executed along with Yang Jinying. Even the consort who had known nothing of the plan was executed. Ten family members of Jinying were killed and 20 were made slaves and sent to the bitter reaches of the north. It was said that when the young women were executed, a fog spread throughout Beijing and remained for four days. The fog lay thick and grey upon the ground, so thick that no one could move about the city. People said it was a complaint from the heavens for the injustice of the executions.

The Emperor himself remained blind in the left eye and disfigured. He never left the Palace Grounds afterwards and admitted only his most trusted counselors to his presence. He lived a long time and ruled for twenty-five more years. He was known for the stupid trust he placed in one of the most malign ministers in history, the Grand Secretary Yan Song.

The Grand Secretary and the Obscene Book

Six hundred years ago, in the time of the Ming, all the greatest Confucian officials came to work each day at dawn; through the high walls of the Forbidden City, they proceeded to their tasks. Some set to work in the offices near the outer wall; they reviewed documents coming in from the far points of the Empire. Some officials were still more grand; they worked in the middle compounds: drafting legislation, channeling the finances and setting the examinations. But some worked deep within the innermost compounds, by the altars, temples and Imperial audience halls, even where the Emperor lived. These great men advised the Emperor in council, censored the corrupt, and wrote the histories of their times. As an official walked through one compound and then another, gate by gate and hall by hall, into the innermost chambers, it seemed his rank increased step by step.

Now, the most highly trusted official was the Grand Secretary. His power was supreme among all the others; he alone could penetrate from outside the walls all the way to the side of the Emperor, from the profane world into the sacred halls; and much depended on his character and wisdom. But during the Ming Dynasty, there was one Grand Secretary named Yan Song whose corruption knew no bounds. He served the Emperor Shizong with special zeal; he stood near the Emperor, advising him each day, and headed the vast bureaucracy, writing the laws and determining the punishments. He monitored all reports and all rituals and his power was supreme. In his own grand carriage, from his own great estate he rode to the Palace, to walk through the massive gates, compound by compound, to arrive finally by the Emperor's side.

But Emperor Shizong was an average sort of man, earnest at first, but, finally, a bit ordinary. Though he made an effort to govern in his youth, by the time the troubles of his rule had increased, he had become a remote devotee of Daoist Arts. So the Emperor's Secretary, Yan Song, was accorded more power than any grand secretary had ever had before; with a venal eye to his own power, Grand Secretary Yan Song amassed a huge fortune for himself as well as for his own fat, one-eyed, hunched-

back son. He took bribes for every position awarded, raked in payoffs for the great Imperial projects, interceded between Emperor and his ministers, and punished with savage brutally those who opposed him.

There was one man, however, who fought Grand Secretary Yan Song. The great scholar Wang Shizhen despised the man. He deplored Yan Song's odious mien, abhorred his venomous schemes, and loathed the Grand Secretary's sycophants and toadies—and he made no secret of his corrosive disdain. Wang Shizhen announced to his friends: "Grand Secretary Yan Song violates the bond between ruler and subject, steals from the Imperial Treasury and tilts the empire aslant; he shakes the Court to its very foundations." Now Wang was a man of great literary skill. He wrote poetry and essays, histories and plays. He was a brilliant man of the age, known for his wit and scholarship; so Yan Song feared the words of this great scholar; and it was only a matter of time before Yan Song would seek revenge.

Wang Shizhen's own father was himself a great official, in charge of a punitive expedition to the Northern borders. But in the military campaign against the border peoples, there was a decisive battle, and the Imperial army was defeated. The Grand Secretary Yan Song now saw his chance; he castigated Wang Shizhen's father before the Emperor. Close by the ruler's side he declared that the father must be executed. The Emperor Shizong was a silly man, a bit stupid, and, finally, uninterested; of course, he agreed. Wang Shizhen pleaded with the Emperor; he petitioned for his father's release, and submitted remonstrances. He argued fervently for commutation of the sentence and wrote memorials to persuade the Court: but—all in vain. In 1560 his father was executed.

Wang Shizhen could do nothing, all his fine words and brilliant writing, his delightful plays and witty essays, his profound poems and acerbic tales, his careful histories and measured observations—all his scholarship and letters were all as dust to him. He was helpless. But the will of the pious is not stopped by fear. Wang Shizhen swore by the altars of the Confucian Temple that he would stop the Grand Secretary Yan Song by any means possible.

One day as he sat in his study surrounded by his scrolls and books, Wang Shizhen devised a plan to avenge his father's death. He called his neighborhood granny and sought her advice. She said she would return in one year with the solution—as it would require all her skill to decoct what he wanted. Wang, meanwhile, wrote a book, a special sort of book, a book just for the Grand Secretary Yan Song. It was a book filled with lust and envy, a tale of women and men, concubines and courtesans, corruption and greed—one hundred chapters of all the aberrant and ignoble, the obdurate and sad, for Wang knew that Yan Song loved such books.

And Wang told no one but the granny.

One year later the plan was ready, and Wang met with his granny accomplice. She had completed her first task, and now she must complete another. Wang gave her the commission; she must somehow, as if by magic, deliver that book. She must ever so discreetly, by hook or by crook, in the greatest stealth and by the most secret means, transmit the pages with all their venom, far into the palace, deep in the successive compounds, so that, finally, even within the Emperor's own sanctum, there would suddenly appear on the desk of the Grand Secretary all those oozing chapters. And no one must know who did it.

This, of course, was easy for the granny.

One morning, as Grand Secretary Yan Song sat down to his desk he found a great, big book—in one hundred chapters—*The Plum in the*

Golden Vase. Taking it up without suspicion or fear, here in the security of the palace, Yan read the first chapter. He could hardly put it down—the first chapter flew by. He couldn't wait to read the next chapter the next day; and quietly, in the privacy of his study, he set aside the reports and the laws, and read of the sensual pleasures and sexual depravity of the household of shame. He read of Golden Lotus' seduction and the murder of her husband; he thrilled at the scenes in the courtesan house with the girls of thirteen; he sat upright by the window, raptly following the terror filled death of the master of the estate. "What a delicious book," he thought, as he turned the pages.

Finally, one hundred days later, as the world of the book seemed to sweep over him with more clarity than his own world, Yan Song realized his body was wasting away. His lungs were weak, his stomach sustained no food, his eyes were watery and dull, and his voice, once so powerful in court, was a brittle, crackling rasp. Though he sought advice from the Palace Physician, he was doomed. His life force was too weak. By the last page, Yan Song was dead; and no one in the Court knew how.

Of course, Wang and the Granny knew. They had cultivated Yan Song's taste in reading. The avenging son had carefully placed a toxin decocted by the granny at the top left side of each and every page of the obscene book. When Yan Song moistened his finger to turn the page, always eager, always hurried, he consumed the poison in precise doses, and Yan Song succumbed, finally, to a fatal case of reading.

The Annoying Ghost

Master Li grew up in a small town not far from the great city of Hangzhou. To prepare for the examination, his family sent him to live

with a famous scholar in the nearby city, hoping he would acquire the skills necessary to pass. Finally, after six years, the tutor determined that Master Li was ready, and the young man set off for Beijing to take the great exam to gain entry to the bureaucracy. He loaded the books, clothes and supplies he would need on his little houseboat and set off on the journey north. On the third day of his trip, just as he was untying his craft at a small town on his route, a Mr. Wang—his old neighbor from his village—appeared at the door of the cabin, and asked to join him on his trip to Beijing.

"You are welcome to join me, if you are not in a hurry," agreed Li. "Indeed, I would be pleased with your company."

The two traveled the next day and, at nightfall, Li anchored the boat and ordered a meal from the vendors at the shore. As they sat down Wang suddenly said to him with a smile: "Now let me ask you something."

"Please do," said the host, as he opened the covered dish.

"Are you of a timid temperament?" the guest pursued.

"Why, no," Li replied, looking up from his bowl.

"You frighten easily then?" Wang remarked as if concerned.

"I can assure you, no," replied Li, as he set the dish down on the table.

"Then," said Wang soberly, "you think of yourself as confident, even brave perhaps?

"Oh, this is silly," Li said, giving up on his food.

"It's not that serious," said the guest, with a wave of his hand. "But I just wanted to make sure."

"Well?" Li said, sounding weary of the matter.

"I'm a ghost," said Wang.

Li sat back very quietly against the far side of his boat.

"There!" said Wang with a smile. "I'm glad to see that didn't shake you up too much."

Li was very still for some moments and then asked his guest calmly what had brought him to such a pass.

"Well, I'm afraid that since you left six years ago to study," his old friend said, "I have had a number of problems. As I'm sure you know, our clan had a fine ancestral temple in the middle of our property, and it was my job as eldest nephew of the head of the clan, to maintain the accounts and keep the household strongbox. Well, I embezzled money from the clan and stole from the strongbox. Then, to cap it all off, I knocked down the old man who guarded the hall and—wouldn't you know—he struck his head on the stone step and died. Then I fled our town and hid in Beijing where I stashed the money near the Temple of Heaven. So to be brief about it, I embezzled and stole, I violated the family altars, oh, and I murdered: although it was an accident! For all that I was tried and executed.

"This is ghastly!!" said Li. "I can hardly believe my ears."

"I'm not finished," continued the ghost. "When I was eventually executed I was sent to the realm of the dead and sentenced to The Burning of the Five Viscera and The Suspension Head-First in the Vat of Excrement. My only hope is to get my sentence mitigated—but only if I return to the altars of the clan, return the money, and, absolutely, face to face—before each and every spirit tablet of my clan—make a profound, full and complete acknowledgement of the vile and despicable acts I committed. If not, why then it's an eternity in the Vat for me!"

"I don't like the sound of that," said Li.

"I don't either," said the ghost. "But that is why I must—in person—return the cash I stole to the clan altars back in our hometown, and the

64

sooner the better."

Finally, the boat arrived in Beijing and Ghost Wang set off for the city. After but a few days he came back to the boat, and, with a bounce in his step showed off the stolen gold he had hidden. "I'm ready!" Said Wang. " I've got the money back. Now let's get going!"

"Well, now just a moment," said Li. " I'm here for the examinations."

"Well, this may come as a shock to you," said the ghost. "But, as it turns out, you're not going to pass."

"I AM going to pass—should my ancestors wish it. And I AM going to sit for the examination!"

"I'm only trying to help," said Ghost Wang peevishly.

"Thank you," Li said coolly.

Finally, after a week of preparations and registration, Li sat for the examination. After the fifth day, the grueling series of tests came to a welcome end and Li returned to his boat.

"Excellent," said Wang, when the candidate returned. "Sit down right here and let's plan for our dawn departure."

" 'Our dawn departure' will be in two weeks hence—after the results have been posted," said Li.

"Well, as a matter of fact, you haven't passed," said the ghost with a shrug. "So I can't imagine why you think you need to wait for the results."

Li didn't know whether to be furious or miserable. "Look," he said in frustration, "the results are in two weeks. Surely you can wait!!"

But, sure enough, when the results were posted, Li's name was not on it.

"Now, I suppose, you're ready to go?" Said Ghost Wang.

Of course, Li was deeply disappointed, but he was also embarrassed, for he felt he had kept the ghost waiting for nothing. And so, Li finally set off for home. Four days into the journey the two travelers pulled up to the little canal side town of Suqian.

"You know," said Ghost Wang, "I haven't had a bite to eat since the last ghost festival, may I suggest we go off to the festival at the City God Temple. There may be a sacred drama on the schedule. Even here in the provinces they can be amusing." But after a few episodes, the ghost disappeared and Li was left to himself. He waited a bit after the play ended, expecting the ghost would show up, but then gave up and went back to the boat.

Suddenly, the troublesome fellow came running back breathless—with that odd wheezing sound ghosts make when they're breathless; but now he was all dressed up in a magnificent outfit—brocade crimson with green jacket—and gold helmet and a handsome sword.

"Good-bye," said the ghost. "I'm not going back. I'm staying here."

"What do you mean, you're not going back?"

"Not going back—Not going back—I'm not going back! I've been given a job. Look at me! I am to be the new God of War for all the important state and county festivals. Just this evening, when we were at the temple I saw the City God in a complete state. I can not tell you!! The God of War Temple, the most important temple in the town—after the City God—had some snipe of a demon, some ruffian of a petty criminal, executed for violations of the tax code. This miserable excuse for a ghost was serving as the god in the festivals. When they put these robes on him he looked ridiculous!"

"I suppose he was making a mess of it," Li said with some concern.

"You have no idea."

"So they decided to give it to me. I can tell you I won't show up late or cause problems or look like some nobody from the hills," he said smoothing out the front of his jacket.

"But what about the money??"

"Oh, you can take it back," the ghost added confidently.

"I thought you were doomed to The Burning of the Five Viscera and The Suspension Head-First in the Vat of Excrement if you didn't return to the altars of the clan, return the money, and absolutely, face to face, before each and every spirit tablet of the clan acknowledge your vile acts?"

"Well now, see here—you wouldn't deny a fellow a position? A job's a job, you know. You can't just walk away from opportunity."

"But what about all the, you know, profound full and complete ac-know—"

"Let's be realistic," interrupted the ghost. And then, giving Li a knowing look, he handed Li the sack of money, "I'm sure they'll take the cash."

With these words, the ghost bowed his thanks and disappeared.

Mr. Li stood on the riverbank for a moment, and with a small sigh, boarded his little boat. The canal trip south was an easy few days, and after returning to his own village, he dutifully, in the way he always did things, returned the sack of gold to the elders of the Wang clan. Then, though still disappointed at his failure in the exams, he was happy enough to make his own way back home to his family.

Followed by Good Ghosts

During the Yuan Dynasty there was a wealthy farmer from Shandong called Yuan Zishi; he lived with his wife and sons near the town of Ji'an, not too far from the base of the great sacred mountain called Mount Tai. Every year, in gratitude for his crops and for the stable and prosperous home, he made a pilgrimage with his entire family to Mount Tai to honor the Great Mountain God, as well as the other Spirits who ruled from Mount Tai. Like many a believer from all over China, he prayed to the Mountain God at the Daimiao temple at the base, and at the top he worshipped the Goddess of the Azure Clouds, to pray for the health of his children; and along the way he made offerings at the temple of the Jade Emperor, the Divine Judge who insures that the wicked are punished in the Court of Hell.

Now, in his town, was a Master Miu, a merchant who had known Yuan since the two were children. Miu was a good businessman, but, because he had lost four shipments of grain, he was in danger of losing his business. In a desperate state of mind, Miu went to his neighbor, Yuan Zishi, and asked for a loan. Of course, Yuan agreed, and he loaned the merchant two hundred ounces of silver. Miu was greatly relieved and deeply grateful. "You are a virtuous man," said Miu. "Now, do not worry. I will repay you by the next festival dedicated to the Great God of Mount Tai. Then we can celebrate together with a pilgrimage to the top."

Now it came to pass that the Yuan Dynasty was coming to an end, disorder filled the land and the prosperity of even a rich province like Shandong was threatened. But Merchant Miu foresaw the troubles, and moved far to the South, to the prosperous region of Huizhou. There he

Shandong

made a fortune for himself by hoarding supplies and running up prices, increasing his holdings ten-fold. But in Shandong in the north, bandit raids increased and even the devout Yuan Zishi suffered five years of losses. Finally, when disorder and famine ruled the north, Yuan too made his way south to Huizhou with his family.

In the city of Huizhou there was a temple dedicated to the God of Mount Tai; so Yuan settled nearby and got a job sweeping floors and tending the rooms of the Temple. His only comfort in that strange place was the companionship of a Daoist priest who tended the shrines of the temple. Together they would enjoy the stories and plays presented on the holidays, as well as the rituals and prayers. It all reminded Yuan of his old home in Shandong, and of the great vistas of Mount Tai he had, so often, visited.

Now Yuan knew Miu was in Huizhou and he longed to see him, but his torn and miserable clothing shamed him. At last, however, no longer able to face his family's sad state, he plumped up his courage, and went to visit Miu to reclaim the loan. Miu received him with courtesy, offered him tea, but said nothing about the loan. Yuan Zishi then made two more calls, but other than a cup of hot wine and some snacks, he came home with nothing.

"You have made three calls and have seen nothing but some conversation," his wife exclaimed. "Are we to starve while he returns your silver with a pot of tea?"

Yuan knew he must press the matter forward; so, bracing himself for the discussion that he knew must take place, he paid a fourth call on Miu.

"Of course, I have not forgotten the matter of the money you loaned me," said Miu as soon as they sat down. "But you know I must have the

note of credit, then I'll pay you back at once."

"But we are of the same village, we grew up together. What note of credit?" said Yuan, with a fear gripping his stomach. "I certainly made no mention of one when you needed the silver, why do you mention one now?"

"Please, sir, let us calm ourselves," said Miu. "If you do not have the note, you must allow me an extension while I attempt to clarify the matter. But," Miu said coolly, "I think that you must make an effort to find that note."

Yuan Zishi returned home devastated. His family was in despair and they could not imagine surviving in their present state.

Yuan returned four more times to the merchant requesting his money, but Miu fobbed him off with increasing expressions of contempt. Finally, a year passed and the fall rains moved in. Their little hut was damp and miserable, and the two boys were thin and sickly.

On one of the coldest days, with no coal to burn, Yuan grew frightened. He returned to Miu's estate and threw himself on the ground before the merchant. "Sir!! I beg you!" said Yuan. "As a countryman, have pity on me!! My wife and family are shivering with cold and the wolf of hunger gnaws at the door. I know that you will not repay the loan, but surely you can give us something to keep us from the brink of death."

"Here," said Miu, gesturing to his calendar. "In ten more days we celebrate the New Year. I will send two hundred weight of rice from my own rice-salary as well as two bank notes. Then you will have something nice for you and your family at New Year. Go home now. My servants will bring it to your house."

When New Year's came, Yuan tidied up the house, and he and his wife dressed properly to sit and receive the gifts. He sent his two sons to wait outside the door to announce Miu's servant. Suddenly the two boys came dashing in. "Here he comes!" But the man they saw only continued by without a look in their direction. Then came another man passing by the little hut. This time Yuan ran out to him, thinking he had missed his address.

"No sir, this is for District Officer Li," said the servant, and he continued through the alley. The same thing happened several more times, and finally, with his table bare and his family ashamed and hungry, Yuan knew that he had been cheated. As he stared around him at the bare walls, his wife and children burst into tears.

Yuan could no longer contain his fury.

That night, as his family slept, Yuan sat for hours, sharpening the broad cleaver from the kitchen, watching out the window, as he waited for the dawn. When the night watch sounded its last drum roll, Yuan set off for Miu's house. At that hour, not a soul walked the streets.

Only Yuan's old friend, the Daoist priest—who maintained the shrines at the Temple of Marchmount Tai—sat awake by his little front gate. Although deep in his ritual chanting, he still heard Yuan's footsteps as he came by his door. Looking up, the priest was astounded to see his friend Yuan followed by a throng of ghastly demons; at Yuan's left shoulder was a bug-eyed, scowling demon in green, and at his right was a squat and drooling goblin. On behind them trailed a retinue of creatures, naked, scarred, twisted, and shaking, all carrying weapons.

After a while, just as the priest was finishing his chanting, he saw Yuan coming back, now heading for home. But now, the Daoist saw a completely different retinue.

A group of happy, handsome soldiers, some with golden helmets and jade badges trailed behind him. Several carried flags and banners;

73

some bore shining shields. They all seemed peaceful and calm and their expressions were joyful. The Daoist could not understand what he had just seen and had to assume that his friend Yuan had died. Finally, the old priest finished his ritual reading and hastened after Yuan to find out what had happened.

"My friend," said the priest, "tell me what has happened!"

Yuan turned as he saw his friend and stood for a time, as if steadying himself. Then he heaved a deep sigh and gave his friend the details of his encounter. "At dawn I left my house determined to slay that vile man to avenge the wrong done to my family. But when I got to his door I realized that, though I could wreak revenge for the injustice done to me, yet could I not harm his aged mother nor his sons or his daughters who have done me no harm. If I killed merchant Miu surely I would be guilty of taking their livelihood and bringing them to the pass I am in now. So, as I got to his gate, I stopped, the cleaver fell from my hand, and I came back."

The Daoist bent low before him and said, "You sir, will surely enjoy great happiness. For a divine vision has revealed this to me. I saw it all. When you sought revenge you were accompanied by the most malign alliance of demons. When you realized the truth, good ghosts followed you, just as shadow, in sunlight, follows the body."

Yuan realized then that his fate had changed. He knew that though Miu had made an oath to him, and though he had struggled bitterly to hold him to it, yet this oath was best forgotten. And so Yuan Zishi abandoned his claim to the debt and took his family off to the mountains to eke out a small living on a hillside away from the man he so despised. Of course, Merchant Miu was only too pleased to learn that Yuan had forgiven the claim and left Huizhou. Now the two hundred in silver would

never be repaid and he counted the abandoned debt as a fine new asset. Pleased with his bookkeeping, he made a visit of thanks to the temple of the God of Mount Tai who sees all the Empire in one glance. The merchant promised the God that, come the God's festival, he would repay him with a great feast.

But the time of the festival came and passed, and Miu forgot the feast, for the dynastic troubles had spread all the way to the south, and Miu was frightened. He worked late into the night, selling and trading, storing and shipping to make sure his wealth remained safe. One night, however, long after the holiday to the God of Mount Tai had passed, the God himself appeared to the merchant in a dream. "Your wealth is safe, I see. But where is my celebration. Didn't you promise?"

"Most Revered God, I am in dire straits now! Perhaps next year? After all," added Miu slyly in his dream,"I don't believe I signed a note."

"Oh, don't concern yourself," said the God pleasantly. "I can still reclaim the promise you made me."

When Miu awoke in his sumptuous bed, he seemed still to hear his own false words echoing in the room, but got out of bed and went to call his servant from the room beyond. When he opened the door, a dreadful sight met his eyes. The most fearsome bandit in the province stood before him, smiling. His wild hair smelled and his naked chest gleamed with sweat. His snarling henchmen were loaded down with Miu's goods—his wealth, his receipts, as well as his daughters—and his sons and servants lay dead in the halls. With nary a look over his shoulder the bandit slashed Miu in the throat and Miu fell to the ground dead, with a look of horror frozen on his face.

When Yuan Zishi heard of the troubles in Huizhou, he counted himself lucky to be quietly safe in the hills. In fact, with cautious care of his few resources, he managed to keep his family from hunger. He used these years of privation to teach his sons; and he and his wife prepared them for service once the Empire was again righted.

When the Ming was established and Han rule returned finally to the land, the two young men became fine officials who never forgot the lessons of poverty. Nor did they forget the lesson learned in Huizhou—that, though a man may owe you some great sum and treat you with vile contempt, yet to shrug off such connection, and forge therein your own success, is worth far more than any hundredweight in silver.

Words in Blood

Lian remembered the way his father had stood beside him in the great temple yard, both of them stilled by the sound of the ceremonial bells. While his father served in Shandong, the boy had gone often to the famous town of Qufu, Confucius' birthplace, to see the ritual dancers and hear the elegant harmonies of the fine choral pieces at the temple. Lian recalled the way the echoes filled the grounds; the immense beams and tall pine seemed to draw the sounds upward into their high shadows. He remembered the procession of Confucian officials in luminous silks carrying the flickering torches in the deep of night. No sight was more potent to the boy, no sight better served to instill in him the high seriousness of a Confucian official.

Now Lian Zining was a grown man; he had taken his own position in the Imperial bureaucracy and become a Hanlin Academician in the court of the Ming Emperor Taizu. There he advised the Emperor of the new dynasty and set to the tasks of instituting the Confucian Rites and the Confucian Five Relations so that the Sub-Celestial Realm would be ordered by humane government. Lian was a dedicated official, always remembering the words his father had cited to him from Mencius: "If, when I examine my heart, I find I am not upright, I will walk in fear of even the poorest man in ragged garments! Beware, beware, what proceeds from you will return to you again."

It came to pass, however, that when the first Emperor of the Ming died, his fourth son usurped the throne and stole the royal crown from the Emperor's eldest grandson. The Emperor of Eternal Joy killed his nephew, the second Emperor; the ruthless uncle trapped his own nephew in the Imperial Study and set it ablaze; then he claimed the throne for

himself, becoming the third Emperor of the Ming.

Lian Zining was in the temple library when he heard the news. His best friend and ally at court, Fang Xiaoru, found him at his study table. The two men spoke calmly. They did not agitate over the report, but assessed the Imperial impiety with deep sadness. The royal lineage was a divine lineage, linked by magical bonds to the sacred ancestors, carried out according to the decorum of the Rites. Even the Son of Heaven obeyed; indeed, as sacred descendent of the sacred ancestors, he was the chief officiant of the Rites.

Now the lineage of the throne was scarred by murder; the ancestral altars were bloodied. Lian and his allies feared the ancestors would rain down punishments; floods, earthquakes, droughts would come. If they sanctioned inheritance by assassination, they would sanction sacrilege. Fang Xiaoru and Lian Zining had no recourse; they could only refuse.

When the Emperor learned of their refusal he was enraged. Their mutinous disputes were an offense, their virtuous claims an insult. He owned the throne; the royal lineage was for him to govern. "This, the 'Great Matter,'" he growled, "obtains to my family, and my family alone."

First the Emperor summoned Fang Xiaoru to court. Fang stood in the court with brush and paper, as he had stood many times before. The Emperor gazed at him in seething fury. Then, gathering his royal robe, he swept down from the dais to stand by the official's side.

"Here is my proclamation," said the Emperor coldly. "You will write as I dictate. You will write that I am Emperor."

But Fang, like Lian, had witnessed the solemn rites of the Confucian temple and studied the Way of the just ruler. He saw here only a terrible impiety. Fang looked down at the brush and let it drop to the floor.

"If I must die," he responded, "so be it. I do not take up the brush for this."

The Emperor shook with anger, and turned to the Imperial guard. "Take him to the execution ground—death by dismemberment!"

Fang was killed within the hour.

Then the Emperor summoned Fang's friend, Lian Zining.

Lian stood before the Emperor as his friend Fang had stood.

"I will be Emperor—and my officials will proclaim it!" the Emperor shouted to the Court.

Lian then spoke with the humility taught him by the teachers of the Confucian Temple. "I serve the Ancestors, and by my official oath I pledged my virtue. If I salvage your ambitions and serve the winds of politics, how can I face my own ancestral altars? Through murder and villainy you have defied the sacred lineage. How can you be the Son of Heaven?" Lian looked around the court as if to search for someone: "Where is the rightful Emperor; where is the true Crown Prince?"

Lian too dropped the brush and refused to write the proclamation. The Emperor was beyond rage, beyond anger. He, who had stolen the throne through murder, shook in fury that his officials should defy him.

"Cut out his tongue!" The Emperor shouted.

Swiftly his guard grabbed Lian and savagely sliced deeply into his mouth. Lian buckled to the ground, doubled over on the stones, blood spilling out between his lips.

The Emperor leaned near to him. "Now will you write that I am Emperor?"

Lian Zining put his hand to his mouth to stop the pain, but then carried the blood from his mouth to the floor. With his eyes clouding over he wrote steadily on the ground, with his own blood, before the Emperor's

81

feet. Stroke by stroke, in measured order, in shining vermilion, the words showed clearly on the stones: "Where is the true Crown Prince?"

But Lian was, like Fang, taken to the execution ground; and so were the members of his family and associates to the tenth degree of relationship. Even his students and their families were killed, for the Emperor's anger knew no bounds.

But the words on the stones could not be removed. "Where is the true Crown Prince?" remained, as clear years later as when first written. Officials would copy them; servants and eunuchs would refuse to look on them. At night they were especially ominous; they shone with an unearthly glow, and they remained there until the palace stones were dismantled and moved to the Emperor's new capital in Beijing. They were placed in a dark corridor, where the shapes of the words could barely be detected.

PART 2

Yangtze Delta

The exorcist holds in his hand a branch of the peach wood that opens the universe; there is the snap of the metal whip, and he is then on the road leading to the Baleful God Star-Jupiter. The exorcist says: Pitiless Star-Jupiter, accept my offerings, and let all the Star-gods come—all the Baleful Stars and the Ferocious Demons, and the Auspicious Stars as well. Then the exorcist proceeds through the Three Gates and enters the Office of the Great Star-Jupiter and he says: "The Divine Lord of the Jupiter Star is truly impressive. Without a very serious reason, I would not have presumed to come."

"The Song of the Visit to the Palaces" an exorcist's handbook,

Taiwan, Hou Ching-lang, trans.

Hangzhou

Crazy Ji

Over a thousand years ago, during the Song Dynasty, the most renowned teachers of Buddhism expounded the Law at the Inspired Isolation Temple in the hills behind the Imperial city of Hangzhou. This monastic compound was famous for the strict teachings of Chan, or Zen. The five hundred monks dedicated themselves to hours of disciplined study, pondered for years the incomprehensible koans, and sat in strictest quietude for days at a time. Pilgrims—grand and lowly—by the thousands came from all over the Empire to worship in the Great Hall of the Buddha and the Hall of the Guardians, and many longed to find enlightenment at the feet of the distinguished Abbot.

One of the most famous of these disciples was a man named Dao Ji; but Dao Ji did not become famous because he could meditate for weeks without moving, nor because he was a profound interpreter of past doctrine. Dao Ji was famous because he was a rollicking, upstart, intemperate, boisterous, happily irreverent drunk. He rolled about on the hillside with monkeys, sang songs with children in the Hangzhou wine-shops and dressed as a clown to shock the Abbot. He talked to the spirits and played tricks on ghosts, and he led his band of followers over house-top-eaves and straight up walls. He was a holy fool who had the power of craziness. He was known, in fact, as "Crazy Ji," or the "Enlightened Drunk." But Crazy Ji was especially famous for a crazy sort of prank he did all the time: a prank that even by Chan standards was outrageous. It first happened when Crazy Ji was but a young acolyte at the Inspired Isolation Monastery above Hangzhou.

One day, amid the many great and noble who came to the monastery, there was one visitor who especially honored the Abbot. This noble pilgrim was none other than the Empress Dowager herself, the august mother of the Emperor. Now, the Mother of the Emperor was a devout woman and a great benefactress. She studied with the most famous Abbess of the capital and sponsored great works to advance the faith. She sponsored important mystics to spread their teachings, and established temples to sustain them. She donated thousands for temple renovations and paid for the sacred play cycles performed by opera troupes. She was deeply dedicated to Buddhism.

One night in a dream the Empress Dowager had a revelation; and so she traveled with her royal retinue to the great monastery on the hillside above Hangzhou. On the road from the lake the long train of royal women met a young monk from the monastery who was sweeping the path in his usual way. Stunned by the sight of the Imperial party he dropped his broom and dashed up the path to the Abbot. "It's a royal party!! There's an Empress! Or maybe a Dowager!" He gasped as he skidded to a stop

before the somber Abbot. The Abbot hastened to prepare himself, and with some trepidation came out to the gates to greet the women.

The Empress was all graciousness. She refused the offers of elaborate hospitality and motioned simply to the party of women—thirty-five strong—to stand quietly as she made a decorous speech. "The other night I had a dream," she said simply. "Indeed, a revelation. In the dream, I saw a Golden Arhat, a saint, who lived now in the world of men as a dedicated disciple of this very monastery. This great saint, now disguised as a mortal disciple, told me of your work, Abbot; but then, in the dream he revealed to me the great hall with the cracks in the eaves, the standing Buddha with the gold flaking off, the libraries with the scrolls now worm eaten and torn, and he told me that, though the goals of the monastery are great, the predations of time had compromised its mission to instruct the world. The Golden Arhat—this saint—revealed to me that fifty thousand in cash was needed to rebuild the great halls and libraries, the shrines and statues of Inspired Isolation. When I awoke from the dream, I was determined to help you."

With that she motioned to a large lacquer chest that sat solidly on the ground among the whispering, long silk gowns and billowing skirts of the palace women. Then, at the Empress Dowager's direction, the Royal Attendant opened the coffer to expose the gift to the temple. Thousands of rosy gold coins lay snugly aligned, strung together by tens, neat as eggs in a row, in the ruby colored satin brocade that lined the lacquer box.

The Abbot was speechless. He bowed deeply, and bowed deeply again, and stuttered out a humble thanks to the Royal Mother, and offered too a spontaneous prayer of gratitude to the All-knowing Buddha and the Bodhisattva Guan Yin, and then to the Bodhisattva of Wisdom

and even to the Bodhisattva of Difficult Studies, and, while he was at it, he offered a prayer of thanks to the four hundred and ninety nine Arhats of the Tiantai mountains, and another to the spirits of the four directions, and, with a last whisper of breath, to the God of Wealth. So many saints and gods were thanked that a great rush of air jostled the candles at the altars. Then he quickly ordered two of his acolytes to approach the Empress on bended knee and then to remove the chest from the Royal Retinue to safe keeping in the hillside vault.

"But there is one thing," said the Royal Mother, with a delicate lift of her fingertips. "I do have a request. Before you remove the royal gift, I must personally thank the disciple of the monastery—the Golden Arhat—who spoke to me in my dream and revealed to me my obligation, and I must meet him in person. I have never, in all my devotions and prayers, met a true Arhat, and I can think of no truer joy."

The Abbot hesitated.

"But of course," he said bowing. "Let me introduce you to the great teachers of these sacred halls. Though none of them has yet achieved the Arhat realm, and all still remain to serve this mundane sphere, yet, I'm sure, one of them must be the Arhat who came to you in the dream. Look, here is Divine Master Zhao, a very holy man. When he lectures on festival days, the halls are filled with pilgrims from all over the Empire."

The Empress Dowager took one long look and shook her head.

"Yes, perhaps his talks are a bit long winded," said the Abbot.

"But here now is Cleric Li: he has cured many with his charms; just last week he exorcised a very malign demon—very malign!!"

The Empress looked away.

The Abbot was abashed and looked about the grounds clasping his hands. Suddenly he gestured to the hallway behind them. "Oh, look!

Coming now from the meditation sanctuary; here is Mystic Liang. He is from an old aristocratic family; his powers of meditation are known far and wide."

The Empress Dowager closed the chest. "Perhaps I misunderstood the Golden Arhat's instructions," she said firmly.

"Let us not be hasty," said the Abbot. "May The Royal Mother pause a while and enjoy some tea from our own plantation." Motioning to the kitchen acolytes, he ordered them to bring out chairs and tables and cups and tea as well as some fine vegetarian snacks to serve the retinue.

When the response was slow and the silence growing awkward, the Abbot nervously turned to the kitchen and barked out, "Where's Ji!!"

Now Crazy Ji was, for all intents and purposes, on permanent kitchen duty. He had tried the patience of the Abbot many times; and many times the Abbot had berated him for his frivolous ways. Unfortunately, on this day of all days, Ji was no more sober and subdued and prepared to take orders than he ever was; and instead of keeping the kitchen fires, he had stood enraptured in the passageway to the courtyard, dazzled by the astonishing array of palace women. He loved the sight of them: the silks of magenta and gold, the patterned brocades of chartreuse and apple green, the gauzy billows of shell pink and smoke blue—and all the beautiful faces, full of youth and sweetness—he saw them all and was as happy as he could be.

Hearing his name, Ji started in surprise; and—coming to his senses—he bounded toward the courtyard. But Ji was never a man for halfway measures; sobriety and decorum were not for him. He could only do what his spirit dictated. He leapt over to the gathering in the virtuoso leaps for which he was famous. And then, like the monkeys he played within the hills, he sprung up into the catalpa tree and swung high from its branches, and then somersaulted down into the retinue.

As usual, Crazy Ji performed his acrobatics wearing just a simple jacket; and, as all the monks and even the Abbot always knew, he wore no underwear. So, as surely as the Buddha escorts us on the final crossing, as surely as the Diamond Sutra leads us to the true path, the men and women of the yard had a plain-view sighting of Crazy Ji's penis. There it was, flapping all about, waving in the breeze, catching the sunlight, amazing one and all.

For the briefest of moments, at the arc of the back flip, the courtyard was filled with an absolute stillness, just as when the halls lay hushed for meditations, just as when the evening summer light catches time in its rays.

But then, it all exploded: a riot of noise and a riot of color. The tidy array of Imperial women and the solemn muster of the Abbot with his monks became as crazy as monkeys on the mountain. The women shouted out, pointing at the sight of Ji; turning to each other, they laughed aloud, shrieking as they clapped their hands to their mouths. Half of them bolted off, dashing into the hallways; they scattered like flower fairies in the wind. It was a blur of fluttering silks and of light, of color and of voices.

The Abbot dashed to the side of the Dowager: "Your Majesty, Your Majesty! Let me explain!!"

But the Empress Dowager seemed unperturbed, and she motioned to the women to compose themselves. Then she turned coolly to the Abbot and nodded in appreciation. "Thank you, Abbot," she said. "Thank you for summoning him. I can see clearly: he is the one." And she opened the coffer once again. Then, with little ado, she assembled her women together and said good-bye to the Abbot.

"Brilliant!" She said to herself as she departed. "Let us never be surprised that all Chan Masters are masters of surprise." And she left.

After that, Crazy Ji never returned to Inspired Isolation Monastery, but continued his studies—or what he called his studies—at the Temple of Jingci, or Quiet Mercy, a temple far less grand and far more tolerant of his strange ways.

The Courtesan and the Immortal

Madam Li was, in her youth, one of the most beautiful courtesans in Hangzhou in the brilliant and prosperous period of the Ming Dynasty. But when she grew old, and could no longer command a great price for her companionship, she established a fine Courtesan Hall at the northern quadrant of the District. She called it "The Cave of the Immortal." It was by all accounts, the best of all the Courtesan Halls. Like the lush estate of a grandee, there were compounds and walled gardens, magnificent plantings and twisted paths, hermitages and studios for painting, poetry readings and private meetings and, of course, miniature mountains and limpid ponds fed by streams and waterfalls.

There Madam Li managed—down to the smallest detail—the week-long parties of Imperial relatives, of powerful officials, of poets of renown, and of the great merchant princes of the South. Of course, Madam Li's courtesans were among the finest; she chose them and trained them so they could match any man in poetry or song or painting. She was an impresario of the highest standards, zealous and successful; but, as she always said, "When the shopkeeper strives, and custom thrives, the God of Wealth looks on and smiles."

Among the most accomplished of her courtesans was Auspicious

Cloud, who, though a mere girl of fifteen, was considered a brilliant diva and accomplished poet. Her parents had raised her to be a courtesan; and since she was five she had been trained by the great poets, painters and musicians of the District. And if some loved her for her brilliance as an artist, just as many loved her for her refined beauty and the ease and grace of her person. Merchant princes of the great clans of the city, rich from trade with the far corners of the world, boasted of the afternoon they spent with her—at tea, that is—if they could achieve a meeting with her at all; for she saw no one she didn't like, and entertained publicly not at all.

As Auspicious Cloud reached her sixteenth birthday, however, it was time for her to find a great patron worthy of her own rank as a courtesan. As custom required, she would spend the night with him, they would become lovers, and the new patron would pay Madam Li a fee worthy of an Imperial visit. "Pick someone handsome if you wish. I wouldn't want you to accept anyone foolish or dull for your first night, but 'Time gallops by like a horse seen through a crack in the wall!'" quoted the madam sagely, "'Don't delay, don't repent.'" But Auspicious Cloud was of a sensitive cast of mind, and she could not be intimate with a man she did not love; so for weeks and then months she put off her choice.

Finally, one day, Madam Li sat down with her in the girl's elegant studio. "Is your life so terrible?" the madam asked. "Few women of the District can choose as you do…but, as we say, 'If fate seals the well, don't cry and die of thirst.' I know that you wish to leave—I did at one time; and turn away from your fate with us here, but remember that, for us of the District—well, you know the saying—'There are three Gettings-Out for the Courtesan: marriage, death, and abandonment.' Do you really want marriage—to be the lowly concubine in the fine house of an old man, locked away, never to see the stage? Think about it. Chose a patron, soon." Auspicious Cloud turned quietly back to her books.

Now, one day, on a fine morning in early spring, a decent sort of man, a young and clever scholar, named Master He, was permitted a few moments of time with Auspicious Cloud. Now, Scholar He was not a rich man, so he expected simply a haughty greeting and nothing more. But the courtesan was charming with him, clearly happy in his presence, as they composed poems together the entire afternoon, finishing finally when the sun's rays warmed the back walls of the garden.

When he left, however, he offered only two copper coins in payment—something much noticed by Madam Li; but Auspicious Cloud seemed not at all to mind. And so every few days he returned and every time they seemed more charmingly matched. Finally, after they had finished an especially happy afternoon, when they had laughed and laughed over a game of chess, Auspicious Cloud said to the scholar: "I must chose a patron, and I have chosen you. I wish you to spend the night with me."

It was as if his fondest wish and his deepest fear had come rushing at the scholar in the same moment. The Courtesan claimed him as her lover, but had asked him to do the impossible. He could no more afford to pay a patron's price for the first rank of courtesan than he could fly to the moon. And what was worse, he was no longer a discrete visitor commanding her attentions in private. He had to accept the responsibility of patron or become nothing. In despair, he said, "I have used every coin I have to visit with you these months—I have nothing more." The two parted in misery.

Wretchedly he found his way back to his little house on a quiet Hangzhou alley, and there he admitted with great regret that he would never afford her company again, not ever. And so Auspicious Cloud was forced to face the terrible necessity of her profession; her scholar was gone and she needed a patron; and though she demurred and delayed as best she could, it was only a matter of time.

One day an odd character came to the Hall—his clothes were humble, he mumbled to himself, and he carried an odd shaped gourd under his arm. But he paid an outrageous sum to read some poems with Auspicious Cloud, and she permitted him to come in. And, in fact, they passed a quiet hour reading a few Daoist poems of seclusion. As he was leaving, however, he reached over to her and pressed her brow with his finger and said: "What a pity!" He then departed as oddly as he had come.

When Auspicious Cloud looked in the mirror that night she saw a peculiar mark, a fingerprint in shadowy rose where the stranger's finger had pressed her skin. And the next morning when she looked the spot it had darkened to carmine red, like a vermilion inkblot, and by the third day it had spread. Within the month the carmine spot covered her cheeks and her nose, and the children of the neighborhood laughed at her. And, of course, she lost her custom—all of it—no chess, no tea, no scholar retreats, no admirers at all. Madam Li was horrified, but could no longer keep her in her elegant rooms to meet the rich. All she could do was keep her to work in the kitchen cleaning and scouring.

One day Master He found himself by the back door of the Hall and came in through the kitchen hoping to get a glimpse of the woman he remembered. There she was in the kitchen over the stove, steaming the dumplings for New Year's supper, with the great red splotch and dowdy jacket. His gut wrenched with pity and he went, without a minute of hesitation, to the madam. "Let me redeem her. I have a bit of land I inherited—surely you can release her to me now."

Madam Li was relieved, and with hardly a word of haggling, saw her out the back door with the scholar, and they wound their way through the alleys, climbing the hill to his studio. But Auspicious Cloud felt ashamed.

"You must let me stay here as your servant, I cannot be your wife." she said.

But the scholar only said: "You loved me when the world loved you, and now that you are alone and in difficulty, you deserve to be loved the more." So they made their home together, far from the great parties and brilliant gatherings that West Lake was famous for.

One day when Scholar He was visiting Suzhou to meet with fellow scholars of his Literary Society, he happened to stay at a little inn on a side street in the famous city. As he sat down for tea, before he went out for his meeting, he happened to sit next to a strange looking man with a gourd. The man introduced himself as Mr. Shi and, hearing that the scholar was from Hangzhou, asked him a question: "Do you know that famous courtesan, Auspicious Cloud? Have you heard of her? Do you know how she is now?"

"But she is my wife, sir—I purchased her registration, and brought her out of the Courtesan Halls."

"How strange," said Mr. Shi. "Tell me, did you pay a great price?"

"No sir, it was nothing really; for she had lost her beauty and was of no value to them."

"How excellent!!" the man said. "So she found the right man after all! Well then, I'm sure you will have me to dinner then when you return home." And with that he left.

Sure enough, Mr. Shi turned up one evening at the little house in the Hangzhou alleyway, clearly expecting a fine repast. When Scholar He found the peculiar fellow at his door, he thought it best to humor him, so he welcomed him in for a simple meal. "Now wait," said the visitor. "Before your wife prepares our dinner, let me fill this basin with the water from my well," and he poured the water from his gourd into the basin. "Bring it back to her to wash her face."

The scholar was of course, surprised, but did as told. He took the little bowl of water back to his wife, who was happily cooking dinner in back, and told her of Mr. Shi's strange request. Now, Auspicious Cloud thought it odd, but did as she was bidden. Bending over the counter she scooped up a full splash of water, closed her eyes, and washed the fresh liquid over her face. She felt her skin tingle and burn. When she stood up, Master He stared at her in amazement; his wife looked, once again, like one of those great courtesan beauties of Hangzhou; one of those finely wrought creatures meant for public celebrations and the private pleasures of great men. She was, once again, exquisite. The two then dashed to the front door to see the visitor, but by the time they got there he was gone.

The news of this strange event spread quickly through the city, and sure enough, Madam Li arrived the next day to see the two. "I don't mind saying that my stage would be much more glorious with you performing, and my wealthy merchants so much more generous; and I would certainly welcome you back," said Madam Li, with a sack of cash placed firmly on the kitchen table. "But I have the feeling that you won't be returning. So I'll leave you two to your private suppers in the still evenings, to your books and paintings on this quiet lane, and to your constant pleasure in each other."

On important occasions Madam Li would return: to help name a new baby—there were two girls and two boys—or to celebrate when Master

He or when Auspicious Cloud published a new collection of poems. And one evening when she came to visit she laughed with delight when she recalled her lecture about the "Three Gettings-out." "I guess there were four after all," she said with a smile. "You found the best one, for, of all the "gettings-out," surely the best one is love." And although Madam Li loved making money with all her heart, she loved it still more when one of her girls defied the odds.

Lady White

On the Spring holiday called Clear and Bright, when the leaves first bud out and before the heat sets in, a young man named Xu Xian went for a stroll in the town of Hangzhou during the heyday of the great Song Dynasty. Now, Hangzhou was famous for the Clear and Bright Festival, for on this day thousands of people gathered in the city, some on horseback or in carriages, and some just strolling along on foot, selling and buying, drinking, eating and visiting. And for those who grew tired of the busy streets in that city of a million people, there were the little islands and flower boats, the hillside temples and pavilions of the great West Lake, whose fresh clear waters lay on the edge of town.

Now, Xu Xian was a handsome young man, a shopkeeper, who enjoyed his life in the richest city in the Empire, and so on this Spring Festival day he took himself off to the entertainment district to watch the acts set up there. The tightrope walkers, the jugglers and acrobats amazed him, and the puppet show and joke tellers pleased him no end, and the riddlers, singers and storytellers distracted him for a while; but eventually, even the animal acts and martial artists, the cavalry displays and sword fights and all the noise and the crowds of the district wearied

him, and he started off to see the pretty shore and fine pavilions of West Lake.

Now, a man like Xu Xian is no different than any other; all he wanted to do was enjoy the amiable breeze on his easy walk by the water, watch a passer-by or two, and, should his luck be right, find himself surprised by love. And, sure enough, this happened. In the slight eddies of the shallow water on the shore of the lake a lovely white water snake looked up and saw him go by. Of course, she was no ordinary white snake, but was a shape shifter-snake—a *jing*—a spiritual emanation; she could transform herself. And this she did.

As she looked up at Xu through the clear water at the lake's edge she fell in love with him. And with no trouble at all, as he turned his back to walk on, she changed her form and became Lady White. Emerging from the wet mud, standing straight as an arrow, she gathered the folds of her skirt around her. Her fine silk jacket and skirt, with the light folds of the fabric—all the shaded overlays of creams, ivories and gauzy whites— framed her discretely beautiful face and made her kind but direct eyes all the more expressive.

As Xu Xian turned to look at her, he fell in love.

Well, in the land of magic, when two lovers meet, nothing stands in their way, and before you can imagine a different ending, they fell deeply and happily in love and were married. So with her faithful ser- vant, "Green Snake"—another shape shifting inhabitant of the watery city—Lady White settled down with Xu Xian. Every day she helped him in the shop; and her gracious manner and clever ways brought him more custom than ever he had before. But the path of these two was hardly smooth, for, as you know, Lady White was not a human at all, but a shape shifter, a water demon, a demon exactly suited to that southern place, a

103

dragon-woman. So she was ever pursued by priests and exorcists, who knew, quite rightly, that to sleep with a *jing* is to sleep with a demon, and that even a loving, elegant, clever demon can get a man in terrible trouble.

One day in the fall, around the time of the Full Moon Festival of Ghosts, Xu Xian was walking past a Daoist temple; there he saw a fine priest, in robe and sash with the cap on his head, lecturing an eager crowd, expounding on the ways of the demonic, chanting terrifying rhymes that could quell even the most secretly hidden of vile demons. But as Xu Xian passed, the priest stopped suddenly and gazed at him. The crowd turned to look.

"Sir, let me see you!" said the priest, beckoning him out of the crowd. "Ah!" gasped the priest. "I do fear for you. Look!" the priest pointed. "I see above you a twist of dark vapor emitting from your head. Your aura, sir, is malign." Xu Xian looked up in fright; but being an ordinary sort of fellow, saw nothing at all emitting from his head, least of all, a dark vapor.

"You need a charm," continued the priest. "Actually, two. It is clear to me that you suffer under the influence of a water demon, and I fear you will not last long." And with that he wrote two elongated characters on two pieces of paper. "Take these with you now and burn them at the third watch, or your manly energies will be drained by her *yin* nature. If you fail, I foretell doom."

Well no one likes to hear the foretelling of doom for his manly energies, and Xu Xian had grown a bit suspicious of his wife when she had given him great ingots of silver with no explanation at all. So Xu made preparations that night.

As the town grew quiet well into the night, and as the watchman

sounded the passing of the third watch, Xu got up and lit the charms on fire. But as the little flames caught the edges of the papers, his wife sat up and stared at him in the dark.

"Xian!" she said intently, a hurt look in her eyes. "What are you doing? Do you actually think me a demon? Have I not loved you deeply?" she asked sweetly, as she grabbed the papers, crumpled them up and tossed them from the room. "Do I not adore you and care for you? And anyway," she continued with some annoyance in her voice, "what sort of husband disturbs his wife's sleep with such nonsense? What is wrong with you?"

"Don't blame me," said Xu Xian. "It was that Daoist priest at the temple by the well."

"Daoist priest!" she said with a sniff.

And she rolled over and went to sleep.

But the next morning she dressed in her most formal skirt and jacket and set off for the temple; and there, as before, was the priest with a similar sort of idle crowd, listening as he expounded on the dangers of demons.

"My, my, my, my, my, my, MY!" said Lady White. "What an idle sort of fellow you are, with nothing better to do than sell your fakery to the foolish! Charms and magic, and even some potions, I'm sure. It's time to keep your foolish magic out of my house."

"I practice the sacred methods," boomed the priest. "The gods of the Northern Dipper and the Spirits of the Five Heavenly Thunderbolts have delivered to me their divine arts. The talismans of my method cannot be resisted. Evil spirits and animal demons, shape shifters and ghosts—all are changed in a flash to their true forms. Be gone, foul creature!" And he set out to burn a Daoist charm. But Lady White seemed much amused by his declaration and, with a wink to the crowd, said she had some little trick up her sleeve that "she had learned as a child," as she put it. And with that she muttered something which no one quite heard and caught the priest buy the collar of his coat.

The priest got an odd look on his face and then began to shrink. Smaller and smaller he got, until he became a squashed up nubbin-man, bobbing about like a kite in the wind. It was all he could do just to scold and shout, pinched between Lady White's fingers, hanging by the collar of his coat. And his big booming voice, so grand before, as he chanted the spell to exorcise demons, turned into something you could hardly hear at all: just a thin, high pitched noise, like the arguments of mice, heard from a distance.

And he was very, very angry. "If you don't let me down, I'll banish you to the Hall of Demons," he squeaked.

"What?" asked Lady White.

"I'll exorcise you—and send you off into the darkest realms of Mount Tai, to the Hall of the Punishing Knives, and the Field of the Pustulous Sores," he peeped.

She gave him a pleasant smile.

Finally, the priest grew exhausted and just hung there.

Whereupon Lady White took the demon bowl he carried and dropped him into it. He caught the rim and slid to the bottom and lay there in a tiny ball of robes and sashes. And Lady White went home to her husband, satisfied that, at least for now, she would not be disturbed by a meddlesome priest who had nothing better to do than tell a woman she had no business being a demon.

The Girl in the Temple

Master Song was an ambitious young scholar from the city of Hangzhou. Like all young men of fine family, he was determined to pass the great civil service exams held every three years at the provincial level. He hoped that one day he would pass all three stages of the exam and bring glory to his family by winning a high post in the Imperial government. But the rigors of the examination were legendary. Locked in a cell for five days, he would have to summon up from memory pages of text from the Confucian Classics, from the Imperial Histories and from the poetry of the masters. And so Song left his home to study in a small temple in the hills behind West Lake. In the cool spring nights he would sit at his desk chanting the prose essays and great poetic lines needed to pass the exams the following year. Night after night he trimmed the wick and prepared his lessons, half listening to the sounds in the quiet back garden. But, though he was dedicated to his studies, he longed for some human companionship.

As if in reply to his unspoken wish a woman appeared one night in the doorway outside his room, and with a brief hesitation, entered. Even in the lamplight in the mountain darkness he could see her features. She was tall and composed, her pale complexion set off by the sheen of her dark green jacket, her lime colored skirt moving delightfully as she entered. "You chant beautifully," she said. "You must be a fine poet yourself."

Master Song was stunned, and not a little frightened, for ghost women were known to appear to naïve young scholars—indeed, they were an occupational hazard, so Song was wary. He questioned the woman closely, knowing she would have to answer him truthfully. "Are you from Hangzhou?" he asked her slyly. "Where is your hometown? Are you visiting in the Temple?"

"Do you think I will bite you?" she asked impertinently. "Here, sit with me. Let's have no more questions."

The girl in green then posed a line of poetry for Master Song, and without thinking Song matched it with his own. Then the couple began to chant lines together, harmonizing with each other rhyme for rhyme. Of course, Master Song knew the old adage: "A virtuous woman is without talent." Only the brilliant women of the courtesan class could display such skill in music and poetic composition, and so Song came to the unavoidable conclusion that this woman was unchaste. But in the quiet of the night with the circle of light falling lightly on her happy features, he was too pleased with her songs. So, as the temple grounds darkened in the night shadows, and the mountain stillness seeped into the corners of his study, the two sang together past midnight. Finally, as they finished one especially quiet poem, Master Song wrapped his arm around her waist and took her to his bed. The two became lovers that night and she stayed until dawn.

Every night, from then on, the girl in green returned to his study; and every night they chanted the great poems of the past and composed their own songs. Master Song had never enjoyed the masterpieces so much, nor felt so stirred by the beauty of the human voice. One night, the girl improvised a tune so achingly plaintive that Song was struck silent, almost immobile, in sober pleasure. The song and her voice seemed to empty him of all distraction, and they looked at each other in the absolute stillness of the darkening room.

Suddenly, with barely a swish of her skirt the girl stood up and went to listen at the door. "Did you hear that?" she asked him.

"I heard nothing," he answered, annoyed that the spell of her song had been interrupted.

"It sounded like a whirring," she said softly; then, almost imperceptibly, as if to herself, she quoted that familiar saying: "When ghosts visit among men, it is the ghosts who fear men." She stood looking down by the window, as if frozen in place by her frightening thoughts.

"Come to bed," he said, and took her hand. She was calmed by his touch and they spent the night as before. Just before dawn he awoke and found her sitting by the bed. "I cannot tell you why," she said, "but I am still frightened. See me to the inner gate this time and watch me as I climb the temple wall."

The girl in green opened the door and let in a shaft of daylight, and then she slipped out. Song watched as she moved along the wall in the pale morning light, but could see her no more after the path turned.

As usual he started back to bed for a morning sleep when he heard her horrible scream. He rushed out into the little courtyard and traced the sound to a spot in the garden. There was no sign of her at all, but, when he heard a kind of whirring sound, he looked down. Trapped in a spider's web was a lovely bee, mottled green, struggling in the web, about to die. He pulled the web from it and carefully carried in to his desk, and, for some terrible minutes, watched it as it lay on the desk shuddering. But, after a bit, it seemed to stir. The bee flew erratically over to the inkwell and brushed its wings in the ink. It walked back and forth on the young man's paper, as if in confusion; but when Song looked at the odd scratches of ink, he saw that it read one word, "Xie," thank you.

The bee struggled on a bit longer, flew weakly out the window, and was gone.

The Garden in the Dream

During the Song Dynasty there was a well-off family of Nanjing named Wang. They had lands all over the Yangtze Delta, but relied especially on their properties in Songjiang. In that region near the coast they owned silkworm lands and a tea plantation and even some few cotton fields. All these lands made the Wang family prosperous; but every year in the fall someone from the family had to travel all the way to Songjiang, down the Grand Canal, to oversee the properties, examine the yields and collect the rents. Of course, in those days travel was easy; boats filled the rivers and canals, and the thousands of shops and inns that sat along the canal banks provided fine food and good wine.

As the season for collections came near, the family patriarch delegated, as usual, his eldest grandson, Dalang, to make the trip. Ever since he was sixteen, Dalang had made the long trip on his own, with the help of only one servant. In his comfortable little boat they would travel the almost two hundred miles of rivers and canals to get to Songjiang: from Nanjing to Zhenjiang, then on to Wuxi, and Suzhou on the Grand Canal, and then—taking to the little byway streams and tiny canals—he made his way to Luzhi and finally Songjiang.

He especially enjoyed the picturesque little towns that marked the route from Luzhi on. He loved the bright flowers covering the dikes and banks in the early fall and marveled over the perfectly arched bridges that mounted even the smallest canals. He watched the sunrise shine in the water and loved to settle into his boat as the lantern lights played in the shimmering ripples. He always enjoyed a chat or two with the townspeople who welcomed him; and since he was a handsome lad, with a humble and kind manner, he was welcome in many a hostelry and tea

shop that lay along the way.

Now, one day in the fall, after he had left Songjiang and was homeward bound, he and the servant passed through one of those towns he loved so well. Gliding along the little river way, he was struck by the beauty of a comely inn at the water's edge. The balustrades that ran along the paths and balconies were a brilliant vermilion, blue flags at the corners of the roofs snapped in the breeze, tall willows sent their vivid yellow leaves wafting to the ground, and the crimsons, reds and rose-colored hibiscus crowded the bank from water side to the trim little windows of the building. He was charmed by the look of it and moored his boat at the dock.

The innkeeper was a man of substance himself, with properties and business in nearby Luzhi, and he greeted Dalang with warmth. "Sit down in the garden, here," he said. "I am sure you will enjoy some of our famous crab from Suzhou and sea perch from Songjiang. They are fresh with the morning catch." Dalang readily sat down to his dinner, and had a sumptuous meal of the products of the province—ending with bitter green oranges, yellow oranges, sweet lotus roots and chestnuts. "I must tell Grandfather of these fine tastes; Nanjing is not so far that we couldn't ship them there," he thought to himself.

But, as he was finishing his meal he realized he was not alone. Turning from his plates and platters, he saw a face looking at him through the lattice work window. He could see a young woman standing in the little path beyond the garden wall, looking at him. He was afraid to offend his host with an unceremonious greeting, but, as if compelled by her quiet poise, and in the beauty of that lush setting, he met her gaze.

Dalang finished up his meal and saw that the sun showed half the day gone; he realized it was time to leave; he was, after all, a man of

115

business. So he thanked his host, unmoored the boat, and pulled into the canal to head homeward. The boat moved easily northward, but Dalang could not attend to his task. He seemed to feel only a sharp sense of regret as if he had lost something. That night, he moored outside of Wuxi, and fell into a deep sleep.

In his sleep he dreamed of the inn at the water's edge. He dreamed he went to the young girl's compound and saw her studio surrounded in willows. He walked along the path through the garden, and admired the strange stones behind the small pond. The garden was trimmed and cared with crisp borders and clean stones, polished like a pearl, the greens of leaf and petal stood out to his eyes like a scene from a painting. She took him by his hand and they entered her chamber together: they first read poems, then composed love songs and finally went to her bed.

It was unbearable to wake up in the morning, rocking in the water of the canal, under the tidy thatched roof of his boat, completely alone.

Upon his return home, he made formal greeting to his family, and together they all celebrated his safe return. He reported on the receipts and earnings of the Songjiang property and then went dutifully back to his work and daily studies. But his dreams seemed never to change. Every night he saw the inn again; every night he joined the young woman in her hermitage. Some nights the two lovers wrote poems and some times they played music and sang; and every night they went to her bed. One night as he was about to leave, she gave him a gold ring with a lapis stone and he gave her a jade fan-pendant of two fish.

The next morning as he was sitting down to a light breakfast with his father, he realized he was wearing a ring with a lapis stone. With a shock he recalled the dream from the night before and he instinctively hid his hand under the table. And of course, when he checked his fan for the fish

pendant, it was gone.

The next year, again in the fall, Wang took to the canals to collect the rents. When he came to the bend in the river he looked again for the inn, half-expecting that it would have vanished, fearing that the gracious host, the meal on the patio, the woman by the lattice were all one of those ghostly visions summoned up by the watery powers of the region. But as he looked out from the deck, craning his neck and leaning over the water to catch that first glimpse of the shore, there it was: the yellows of the leaves, the vermilion balconies, the lovely hibiscus on the bank and the blue flags flapping in the autumn breeze: as real as real could be.

This time his host greeted him at the dock. "She said you were returning," said the old man in a rush of words. Wang Dalang was taken aback by this, but sat down and listened.

"I am an old man," he said as he composed himself, "with only a daughter to help me in my old age. But since you were here last year, she declined terribly. She has done nothing but stay abed and sleep, and mutter to herself like a mad person; and the diet and medicine recommended by the Granny have not helped. But today she arose, dressed in her silk jacket and skirt, adorned herself with the sash and jewels her mother left her, and said to me 'He will soon be here.' I thought she was madder now than ever before; but then I saw your little skiff as it came round the bend. Clearly, the gods have arranged this."

Then the two men went back to the young woman's rooms, through the little garden on the crisply curving path, past strange stones and lush greens, into the grove of elegantly pruned willows to her hermitage. There she waited for him exactly as he remembered her, as calm and composed as when he first saw her. They spoke then of the ring she remembered giving him and the jade pendant he gave to her, as well as the poems they composed together. There was no question they were destined to be together.

Needless to say, both families were delighted to arrange the marriage, for they knew that, "what the gods arrange, no man should counter." And, in any case, with the two families joined now in marital harmony, the reach of their properties and size of their rents, the goods and shops they both now owned, and the delicacies they could ship from the coast to Nanjing, all made the union of the two dream lovers even more delightful.

And sometimes, always in the fall, when the two could get away from the family compound in Nanjing to see the wife's father, they would take the little skiff down the southward route of the canal, pick up the byway rivers at Luzhi, and come round the same bend of the river. Almost like children, they would lean out over the water. And as they caught first sight of the old building, still bright in the evening light, they would settle back to see with immense pleasure, the blue flags flapping in the autumn breeze, amid the yellow leaves of the tall willows, that grew through the red hibiscus on the river's edge.

Snowy Night

Wang Huizhi had served in the Qi court as a great official; but his reputation had been marred by his eccentricities and odd ways, as it seemed he much preferred the sounds of his zither and the sight of the graceful bamboos for companionship. So, giving up on all the worry of serving in a time of grievous conflicts, he retired to live as a recluse by the Shan River. In his small house on the riverbank he played the ancient music he loved and chanted the works of the great poets.

One night in the second month of winter, as the light dimmed in the afternoon, a great storm began to blow. The early gusts of sleet turned to a driving snow and the little glimmer of light from the hut showed only faintly in the gathering dark. Forgetting his music, Wang put aside his zither, and heated up another cup of wine. Outside, the wind rushed through the narrows of the riverway and Wang added coal to the stove; as he heated up another cup of wine, and then another, he listened to the rhythmic surges of the storm against the house. Finally, as the lamp burned down, he unrolled his sleeping quilt, crawled inside and fell asleep.

Suddenly, Wang found himself completely awake. Sitting up in the midnight chill, he listened for the storm outside; but instead of the bluster of the wind, there was only an overwhelming silence. Sliding out of his warm quilt he walked to the edge of his room and slid open the panels of the house. The storm had ended, and a brilliant whiteness covered everything before him, from his little hut, down across the river and on beyond to the horizon. Only a few splotches of black stood out in the river as the current churned up the snow. Reaching for his wine from the evening before, he raised his cup in both hands, and said in a whisper: "To the night." As the wine warmed him inside he began to walk slowly about in his room chanting songs.

Taking my walking stick, I search out the hidden recluse,

Seeking out that tangled path that connects the Then with the Now.

All at once Wang stopped his singing as he recalled his dear friend Da Gui—a recluse like Wang—who lived far southward along the Shan River. The two had not seen each other in over a year. Struck by the inspiration of the moment, Wang bundled himself up and headed down the little path to the river. He found his skiff tied to the bank, and despite the

121

chill and the darkness, he climbed in and headed off down stream to Da Gui's tiny village, miles and miles down stream. The snow had stopped completely and for the rest of the night almost till dawn, Wang guided the little boat through the silent white, passing the villages and groves of trees that stood along the riverbank.

Finally, as he approached the village where Da Gui lived Wang was overcome by a sense of the stillness of the place. Easing to the shore, he sat back in his boat and paddled softly, letting the boat drift. He sat for some time in the gently rocking skiff, with his head turned to the side—as if listening to the sounds of the river behind him.

Then, suddenly, he turned the skiff back to the north, glided easily back into the current and began to paddle homeward. He was back by late morning.

Later, he was asked by a friend why he had turned around so near his destination, going all the way back to his hermitage, without even seeing his friend Da Gui. Wang simply told him that he had been riding the impulse of the moment; and when the impulse had left him, what was the point then of going on to see Da Gui?

The Grandee and the Storyteller

By the age of sixty-two, Dong Qichang was at this peak. A great Grandee, he ruled like a potentate in the glittering city of Suzhou. Hundreds scurried to do his bidding—attendants, retainers, agents, stewards—all ruled his estates on his grand behalf. Even the fine mandarins and great clansmen held him in awe, happy to stoop low as they entered the high gates of his estate. And all those fine citizens of Suzhou—all the merchants and artisans, the clerks and shopkeepers, the dockworkers, mari-

ners, tradesmen and students—they feared him: whispering his name when his fine retinue swept grandly by.

But, Dong Qichang was more than grand, he was gifted. He was a master calligrapher, known as the most brilliant artist of his age. His explosive brushstrokes of black ink brought him fame beyond fame. From gentry to aristocrat, from merchant to imperial clansmen, all adored his work. "A true immortal," said one admirer, "descended to us from the heavens." With his artistry, Dong Qichang dallied among the stars of his age, sojourning in the vermilion halls and stately parks of the greatest in the land. Indeed, for Dong Qichang, a visit to an Imperial retreat was like a trip to the local tea house, for his art was his currency, and he controlled the most precious coin of the realm. When Dong Qichang spent a month with a royal relation, all he needed to do to repay his host was compose a single line of characters in his own brilliant style.

But though Dong Qichang was a fine artist, he could not resist the seductions of power, and gradually, over the course of his life, he was made coarse. Always confident of his gilt-edged connections, he slighted customs and defied laws. Hungry for magnificent gardens, he stole the land of his neighbors. Greedy for beautiful things, he bullied and robbed the artisans and merchants. And on his ever-growing estate, he ruled like an Emperor. It was whispered that he allowed beatings, kidnapping and rape.

But despite his arrogance and cruelty, none dared raise a voice. For in these times—in the waning days of the Ming—when the silver of the world flowed to China, the storehouses of the rich brimmed over with cash and the kingdom was ruled, not by wisdom, but by coin. So men like Dong Qichang could disappear in their aura of gold and thread the needle to the coteries at Court. With money and connivance he could buy what favor he required; for justice was—in these times—just another commodity, an item of exchange: coin for conscience, cheap at the price.

One day, as Dong Qichang walked among the back gardens near the women's apartments, he caught sight of a girl standing quietly by one of his red lacquered pillars. She was a slim, little thing, no more noticeable than a stalk of grass. Dong Qichang took a sudden liking to her and found out all he could.

She had been brought in to serve his first wife from the small canal town of Luzhi. Her father was a poor scholar who hoped his daughter would learn fine manners in the great household. The artist was much taken with this sudden encounter, and despite proper family prohibitions, he followed her to her quarters. Catching her about the wrists, he sought to bring her to his own suites, but being the proper sort of girl she was, she struggled from his grasp and darted off. Day after day he pursued her and cajoled her, but always she fled away in confusion and shame.

Finally, when the girl's father heard of his daughter's plight, he grew fearful, and he summoned her back home, giving the excuse of her mother's sickness. But, by this time, the entire household was aware of Dong's desires; and his sons, accustomed to every manner of indulgence due entirely to the great man of the realm, were furious. How could a mere scholar, a poor man, a nobody, in fact, have refused their father his whim. They felt it a great injury to their family dignity.

So they gathered together the factotum Chen Ming, the henchmen of the compound and the guards of the three estates and set out to raid the scholar's little house. Two hundred strong, they swooped into the little town of Luzhi and sacked the scholar's tiny compound, burning, beating, looting and laughing. The little canal city, so peaceful and sober,

was in chaos. The clerks and the merchants, the dock-workers, silk makers, canal men and weavers all ran to help. They whisked the young girl off to the mountains, but the father was beaten almost to death and his little house was in a ruin. The news of the raid spread like a flood, up the canals, and into the great city of Suzhou.

Now, Master Dong Qichang was vexed, for he had missed his chance with the young girl. But he wasted not a minute of thought on the raid itself; and, indeed, there was neither magistrate, nor court liegeman, nor any minion of government, who raised a hand against the great clan. So Dong Qichang—as easy as the sun shifts its rays in his cheerful morning studio—forgot the silly child and settled down to work on more scrolls.

But, beyond the thick walls of the palatial estate, the city of Suzhou stirred; for, though the grandees and officials were as mum as ghosts, the townspeople of Suzhou were not so compliant. They began to talk and they began to complain, and the stories of the old man's pursuit of the girl, of the Dong family arrogance, and of the terrible raid on the scholar's home—all the pieces of the tale—circulated through the city like fog filling the streets in the cool evenings. And if they muttered about the poor girl fled away to the mountains they recalled, as well, Dong Qichang's other crimes: the beatings, the bullying, the secret alliances with magistrates, the abuse, the violence, and the corruption. In a city that ran on business and contracts, laws and agreements, Dong Qichang played as he liked. But the raid on the scholar's house transgressed a vivid line.

It was early in the day, near the Spring Festival, when Old Qian, one of the most famous storytellers of Suzhou, was gathering his usual crowd. Now, Old Qian was from a famous clan of storytellers, famous for generations. These storytellers, however, were not famous for tales of chivalry, nor for tales of battles, nor of fallen empires. The Qian family told tales of Suzhou. Old Qian knew all about the dramas of the house-holds, the successes of the merchants, and the secrets of the Imperial Eunuchs: the legal cases of the magistrates and the troubles of the slaves and workers, and all the conflicts and plots of the fine aristocrats. He was the expert on what happened in this city of three million.

Old Qian had certainly heard every detail of the Dong Qichang affair: the infatuation with the young girl and the terrible treatment of the girl's family. Of course, he was horrified. But, he was, after all, a story-teller, and he knew a good tale when he heard one; and this tale would fill his coffers for a week. It would unfold very nicely, he thought. I'll open with Dong Qichang's finding the girl on his own estate, thought Qian. I'll picture that old man quivering in his official robes as he spies the girl. I'll call the story, "The Tale of Black and White," he mused: Black for the look of the swarthy little scholar, and White for the fancy pen name of the great artist. Yes, thought Qian, he liked that.

Qian began his tale in the middle of the Spring Festival when he knew the crowds would gather; nothing like a good holiday to increase his custom. His tone at first was casual, even easy, as if his tale would amuse; no one would be surprised to hear how the powerful behaved. But as he proceeded, he played upon the details: the family arrogance, the race to Luzhi, the townspeople hastening to fight the bullies, and the fear of the girl as she fled to the mountains. Old Qian swept his listeners up in the twists of the tale.

And the crowd was stirred. By the end of the first day's performance they were restive, by the second they were muttering and looking to left and right, by the third they were standing by their seats and squeezing their fists, and as the last two days proceeded they began to talk: "Come listen—it's all as they said—he has raided the town like the Japanese Pirates. He is nothing but a thief, a bandit, a tiger from the mountains. His clan is a demon clan!"

By the night of the fifth performance the town of Suzhou hardly slept. The townspeople, long silent before the officials and their courtly ways, were in a state of fury. And as the ways of the city would often have it, high and low, student and worker, merchant and even magistrate all took to milling outside the gates of the famous Dong Qichang. Before the dawn they had swelled to a thousand, and as the noon sun warmed the streets, it seemed the entire town was before the gates.

In the evening the grumbling rose to a shout and they cried out: "Murderer!!" Their signs said: "The Beast-Official," and "The Tiger-Grandee." And when the surge of fury could not be contained, they burst through the walls, spilling through the huge gates into the first court-yards, surging forward by the scores and then hundreds into the path-ways and compounds.

At first the crowds seemed amazed. Few had seen such imperial grandeur in their town of business and commerce: the garden and porti-cos, the fine boudoirs and pavilions. But their hesitation was but a second long, as they threw their torches into the fine rooms and burned them all to the ground. Still consumed with rage, they moved through the city to the estates of the sons and on even to Chen Ming's estate. They burned them all and left them in ruins. The clan's great studios and banquet halls, the garden hermitage and fine compounds for the women, even the kitchens and back apartments were smoldering and broken, smoke rising from the embers.

Dong Qichang fled as fast as he could with his sons and stewards to the outskirts, to his farmlands, but the crowd pursued him. Finally, he took to one of his canal boats and fled up river to a home of an aristocrat.

There he remained quietly in hiding for months. Of course, his life was in ruins, his immense household destroyed. Even his sons' estates were in ruins. He was like a poor man, a refugee, a broken old beggar, without a bench to sit on, or a lantern to light.

But as Dong Qichang hid away in exile for months, his allies secretly helped him; his crime was immediately covered up by a friend in the Imperial Censor's office, and no magistrate dared investigate him. And even though his estates were impoverished, still he never lacked a comfortable bed, for all he had to do was pay a call on his powerful allies, who were only too happy to receive him: a month in the retreat of a royal cousin, or a season at the mountain aerie of a great clan patriarch. This went on for years until he re-gathered his riches and properties.

Indeed, it has seemed a good bit of luck for collectors today who pay great sums for his scrolls; for every time Dong Qichang sojourned, he painted another scroll to earn his keep. And since he was—for quite some time—without a home, he painted and painted, scroll after scroll, to show his gratitude. So now, as luck would have it, there are all the more paintings to be had by the rich who seek them out today.

And when Old Qian heard how Dong Qichang had come right after all his troubles, he grumbled to his wife, "I guess the rich can flick off danger as easily as a fly." But then he consoled himself with the knowledge he learned even as a child from his mother and father, something all storytellers know: which is that nothing makes a better story than the tale of a vile and foolish man in a vile and foolish world. And although a fine scroll may be worth millions, still, a good story like that is worth that much, and more.

The Fox Wife

For many years a farmer eked out a meager living growing beans; he had no sisters and brothers to help him, had never married, and so lived alone sowing and reaping his little crop. One day he returned home from his few fields to find his house immaculate; a fire had been laid in the fireplace and a nice hot supper set out on the table. He accepted all this without question, thinking that some visitor from the village had been kind, or perhaps some traveler had used his hut and left the supper in gratitude. But to his surprise, this went on for weeks, and each night the supper, his little hut and even his few torn clothes came to be much improved.

Finally, he could not stand the strange riddle of the secret visitor, so he determined to remain behind a day and hide in the little cupboard he used for his goods. Not long after the time he usually left, the door of the hut creaked open and a small red fox came in. She stretched out her neck and gave a sniff with her shiny black nose; her black eyes considered the hut for a minute and she came in at a trot. Then, like a puppy that rolls to scratch its back, the fox somersaulted over, shed its fox skin and stood up as a lovely young woman.

Immediately, she got to work. She scoured the table and the water buckets, brought in more coal and wood and swept the floor. Then she started the fire and set out the food she planned to cook. As she waited for the pot to boil, she mended some bits of crockery and patched the torn linen that lay on the little *kang*-bed. In a few hours the meal was done, the fire re-laid and the house looked neat and well cared for. "Well, I think that will do," she said, as she ran her hand over the clean table. Then, with a graceful little twist, she spun around down onto the fox

skin, transformed herself back, trotted out of the hut and was gone.

The farmer came out of his cupboard and was both amazed and happy, but angry with himself. "I should have thanked her, or talked to her, or stopped her somehow," he muttered. But he determined that the next day he would certainly say something.

The following day, just after the farmer had tucked himself again into the cupboard, along came the fox to set about her work once again; and, just as before, she surveyed it when she was done. At just that moment, however, the farmer came out of his cupboard and confessed that he loved her. "My hut has been so lonely and you have made me content. I only hope that you will consent to marry me." The young woman was pleased with his eager proposal and she joined him on his farm as his wife. They lived for five years like this and had a little daughter who was as charming and happy, and as pretty and as smart as her mother.

One day the farmer came home from the fields in a poor mood; he was irritated that the crop was late and the water canals almost dry, and he said something sharp to his wife. She was surprised that the farmer could speak so ungraciously and she retorted by saying as much. "Oh you need not take such fine airs with me," he said sullenly. "You are but a creature of the night, a vixen, not even human, I dare say."

She seemed stunned by the remark and looked at him askance. "A fox!" she said in alarm. "We are man and wife!"

"Here," he said. "Look at this." And with that he pulled out from some ancient hiding place the old fox skin.

The wife looked puzzled for a minute, but then seemed to recall something. And with barely a tick of hesitation, she walked over and picked up her daughter in her arms. Once again—as before—she somersaulted down into the skin, now embracing her daughter with her, and

134

stood back up on all four feet as a vixen. Carrying her kit by the scruff of its neck, she trotted out the door of the hut, loped down the path to the fields, disappeared with a swish in the grasses, and, without a turn or a glance, was never to be seen again.

Filled with remorse, the farmer waited for his wife and daughter to return, but they never did.

The Emperor and the Useless Ghosts

After twenty long years of brutal war, the Emperor Taizu drove the Mongols back beyond the borders of China. He established the new Dynasty of the Ming and set to work rebuilding the once great cities of the Empire. Now, the Emperor was much alarmed by the city of Suzhou, for Suzhou was the Venice of China, hub for the other great cities of the South. It sat in the center of a spider web of canals, not far from the mouth of the Yangtze River; barges rolled in from all of China's rivers, and ships sailed in from all her ocean trade to deposit their wealth—silk, porcelain and cotton, tea, iron and wood—on her docks. But Ming Taizu knew that Suzhou was in chaos; there were labor strikes and factory shutdowns, trade stoppages and inflation; prices were so inflated a wheelbarrow of cash was needed to buy a peck of rice. And her famous canals: they were broken down and silted; floods surged over the banks, and terrible epidemics followed the muddied waters.

But the Emperor knew that the taxes collected from Suzhou kept the Imperial armies well fed, so Emperor Taizu attended quickly to Suzhou's disorder. He commanded his brilliant cousin, the great official Zhu Liangzu to lead a commission. So in 1369, within one year of the founding of the new dynasty, Zhu led the Imperial Adviser of the Treasury, the

Chief Attendant of Waters and Seas, as well as the Ranking Officer of Goods and Products along with the Assistant Minister to the Department of Trade to the city of Suzhou to set aright the great city of the South. Setting to work in the ruined official compound, Grandee Zhu Liangzu worked day and night with his officers to quell disorder and establish the economy. He regulated prices and restored wages and stored grain for lean times; he opened docks and recommenced ship building so trade could again expand. He reopened factories and dredged the canals so that shipping might continue apace.

There was one problem, however, which remained elusive. The problem was ghosts; for after twenty years of war, after epidemics and starvation, after earthquakes and ruined villages, thousands of disembodied spirits meandered the land. These "cloud-souls"—remnants of the improperly buried—remained unattended, drifting. Scores of them, indeed bands of them, wandered, without attachment to domestic alters, family gravesites or local rites. In the marshy places, especially on moist nights, they produced eerie and unwelcome noises. Weeping or sad music sounded near the rivers and canals; and in the side alleys and quieter corners of the city, travelers would catch sight of misty apparitions.

Of course, Zhu Liangzu made a full report to the Emperor:

> In the fields around the towns and cities we are especially disturbed. Over three hundred ghosts can suddenly manifest themselves. They gather at all the usual places; some were seen drawing water from wells or at the market places at night, and some are throwing stones at passers-by. And if they are not scattered about in groups, I've seen them standing near the wells in lines.

Needless to say the problem was disturbing; yet no obvious solution recommended itself. The chief exorcist was overwhelmed and the monasteries no longer had priests who could handle such a confusion of ghosts. And no one from the Capital—not the Imperial Adviser of the Treasury, nor the Chief Attendant of Waters and Seas, nor the Ranking Officer of Goods and Products, nor the Assistant Minister to the Department of Trade—offered the least suggestion. And so on it went—more ghosts shuffling by the wells in disconsolate groups and more misty forms shrieking about in river beds.

But one night as he came home late from his office Zhu Liangzu was himself affronted by a ghost. "I cannot tell you what just happened to me," he said to his wife. "One of those ghosts—for absolutely no reason whatsoever—threw a roof tile at me and clipped me right here." He gestured gingerly to his forehead, looking genuinely aggrieved. "I can't imagine what is wrong with them. They are ruining the city, especially at night. They are so disagreeable!!"

"Now, now," said the wife. "What did you expect? You have attended to the realm of the living, but have neglected the realm of the dead. They're not disagreeable; they're just disorganized. Attend to them in the same way you've attended to the canals and factories. It will work out."

So Zhu Liangzu set to regulating the ghosts, these disruptive cloud-souls who lacked proper connections to the living. "Henceforth shall the spirits be organized into categories," he decreed: "By their demise shall we determine their rank." Death by plague, death by suicide, death by drowning or death by warfare, death by building collapse or death by starvation: Zhu Liangzu organized the wandering ghosts by the manner of their deaths, and set down the law of ghost-management. Then for each category he erected altars, that the souls might find the right ceremony to anchor them to the living in an orderly way. No more of this wandering about with no rites to fix them to a place, causing harm to the living in their idleness. In Suzhou City alone he erected seven hundred and forty-one altars. As a result, the ghost problem abated. Fewer tiles were thrown at passers-by and people could safely draw water at their wells. Many fewer ghosts were seen to mill about at will and no one complained of disembodied souls standing about in lines.

Miao Shan

In ancient times Miao Zhuang ruled the kingdom of Xinglin. He was a strong king who had unified the wild tribes of the hill, but his path to power had been bloody, and he held the throne with craft and guile. Now, Miao had three daughters. The first daughter loved fine clothes and delicious food, the second daughter loved the art of the slow ritual dance, and the third daughter was a holy child, dedicated to study and to practices of saintly denial. Her name was Miao Shan.

Like all kings, Miao Zhuang needed an heir, so he commanded his saintly daughter, Miao Shan, to marry his Minister of War, that the marriage might produce a prince. But his daughter refused, for she desired a life of holy works and chastity. Miao Zhuang grew angry at her defiance, and he cast her into the immense Imperial Park and left her there to die. But Miao Shan was happy among the creatures and she began her ascetic path in the quiet days and nights. This made her father still more angry and he ordered her to leave the palace that she might fend for herself in the wide world. But Miao Shan only replied mildly, "I will join the White Bird Nunnery and study the path to perfection." This hardened the King's heart still more, and he went to the Abbess of the nunnery and commanded that his daughter be given all the filthiest chores, for he thought her dedication was vain and her love of saintliness foolish. But Miao Shan carried out her menial tasks, happily scouring, scrubbing and sweeping.

Then King Miao Zhuang was in a fury that she would so defy his power and turn her life on a path to sainthood, and he commanded the monastery be burned to the ground. Yet Miao Shan walked out of the flames unharmed. Then his rage knew no bounds, and this violent man,

Putuoshan and Ningbo

who commanded the armies of the kingdom, commanded that his own daughter should be put to the sword. But the sword flew apart in a thousand pieces when it touched her body. Then he commanded she be killed with a spear, but the spear could not touch her. Then he ordered her execution by strangulation. And when the assassin stole upon her and squeezed the life from her, Miao Shan died, and her soul flew down to the kingdom of the dead. But in that terrible place her soul saw all the souls in torment and she blessed them and rescued them, so that they flew from the circles of punishment up to the heavens, and were released.

Then the Buddha, seeing the devout and holy way of Miao Shan, commanded that Miao Shan be sent on a lotus flower to the island of Putuoshan to become the Sovereign of the Eastern Sea, Goddess of Putuo Island, the reincarnation of Guan Yin. There she healed the sick and salved the tormented and gathered to her thousands of followers.

Now it happened that the God called the Jade Emperor, Judge of Mankind, Ruler of the Dead from his throne on Mount Tai, took note of King Miao Zhuang, and he judged him harshly. "For the crime of murdering your rivals, for the crime of burning the nunnery, and for the crime of strangling your daughter I give you terrible sores." And Miao Zhuang's body became covered with great, pustulous, throbbing cankers, cavernous wounds that oozed day and night. His burning flesh made him mad with pain, and his subjects ran from the sight of him. So the proud king was made low, and for the first time he prayed for help that his stinking skin with the grinding itch and pain might be assuaged.

Miao Shan, far away on the island of Putuoshan, heard her father's prayer, for she was a goddess of healing; and she determined to cure the disease that plagued him. Like the filial goddesses of family cults, she maimed her body to create a divine medicine. In her monastic cell in the monastery of the island, she cut off her right hand and plucked out her right eye. She sent these to her father by divine emissary, that these two bleeding relics of her own body would make the healing salve. And when the salve of the right eye and of the right hand of Miao Shan cured the sores of the king's right side, he was gladdened, yet still he was proud. He looked on the medicine as his just due—as if no divine sacrifice had been made for him. "In the world there are many hands like this," he said.

Yet the sores of the left side continued to plague him and so he prayed again to the Buddha. This time Miao Shan again heard his prayers and she prepared again the terrible cure. From her cell in the monastery, she had her left hand cut off and her left eye gouged out. Again these two bleeding relics of his daughter's body were sent. But this time the king was horrified by what he saw, for he recognized a black scar on his daughter's own hand. "What immortal has sent me this cure? How have I failed to see it was my own child's hand and own child's eye that were sent to me as cure?"

Then, the Goddess Miao Shan appeared to him. She sat before him on a lotus throne with the blood flowing from her wounds and the king was struck dumb with horror. "Now do you believe in the path?"

And the king bowed down flat on the stones of his own castle floor and wept. He renounced the way of violence and accepted the path of the Buddha.

And the Buddha heard the father's cry and heard him renounce his cruel past. So the Buddha granted that Miao Zhuang should himself become a Bodhisattva to teach others of the folly of kingly arrogance. Miao Zhuang became the Virtuous Conquering Bodhisattva, Surveyor of Mortals; and he remained on earth, as all bodhisattvas do, to reveal—to

142

those who have the eyes to see—the true path and the true law. As to the daughter Miao Shan, she took the form of the Goddess Guan Yin, Goddess of the Eastern Sea, and she appears to the faithful who come to the island.

The Old Library

During the era of the Great Ming, when trade from all the world brought wealth to China, there was a patriarch of a great Southern clan name Fan Qin. Fan Qin ruled his estates from the city of Ningbo. He was so rich and powerful that the Ming Emperor called on him to defend the great harbors with his own armada of armed ships; and when Fan Qin was still but a young man, the Emperor appointed him to the court as second-in-command to the Minister of War. There was no corner of the rich Southern region that Fan Qin did not know and control.

But Fan Qin had an obsession; but it was not the cotton and silk he shipped to the North, nor the tea, woods and porcelains he traded with the Japanese and Portuguese. Fan dedicated all the silver he acquired to the one thing he loved the most: books. He bought entire libraries and collected thousands of volumes; he gathered finely copied classics and ancient manuscripts, tomb rubbings and woodblock prints, anthologies of poetry and medieval encyclopedias; and he especially loved the long descriptive histories of each and every region of Ming China. Booksellers and copyists, librarians and collectors lined up by his gates to meet with the great bibliophile.

Now, a library can be destroyed by many predators; and books can disappear over time. So Fan Qin established rules. The five eldest males of the five family branches within the Fan clan retained five different

keys to the library's five distinct locks; and no one could enter without all the five keys present to open all five locks. If one member was found to have entered secretly, he was banned from the next clan worship. If a clan member brought friends or relatives to ogle the collection, he was banned from the clan altars for a year. If someone loaned the books out: banned for three years. And if one page, leaf, scroll or book was sold, the pilferer was banished for life from the clan sacrifices. And Fan Qin enforced his rules.

But Fan Qin's library faced an even greater enemy: fire; for flames feed on papers and silks. With just the smallest spark—a cinder from a kitchen chimney, a neighbor's careless candle—nothing would remain but ashes and smoke, and the walls in the embers. So Fan Qin built the library of brick and tile with no timber in the construction to invite the flames.

But Fan Qin still worried about fire; the collection still needed a safeguard, and something truly potent. But Fan Qin was mystified: what recourse did he have? He thought for months and paced his halls, but the problem confounded him.

Then one night, as he stood among his ancient collection of great prayers and incantations, a solution came to him. He took a scroll from the shelf, then a book, then a manuscript; he examined slowly the legends and myths of the archaic texts, the talismans and charms of the esoteric prayers, all the words and phrases that had been passed down from ancient times. Fan Qin was determined to find the magical words that could stop fire, the phrase that, being spoken, would make it so, and make it safe; Fan Qin was looking for name magic. The name of the library would be an incantation.

And at last he found just the right phrase in an ancient cosmology.

"Heaven's First Power gives birth to the waters," said one ancient text; and Fan Qin was delighted. The phrase was the perfect name for his library. The "Waters" that arose from "Heaven's First Power" would become real waters. Just as the "First Power" calls forth the waters, so will the name of the library call forth protection. The phrase would guard his books. He called his library, the Pavilion of "Heaven's First Power."

Fan Qin died in 1585; but his sons, grandsons and the generations that followed all adhered to his severe restrictions; and the library survived for four hundred years. In 1773 the Emperor of the Qing demanded to borrow his famous books—but even the Emperor returned the copies. Then in 1840 the British stormed Ningbo and threatened to raid the library—but only one volume was removed. Then the Taiping Rebellion brought chaos to Ningbo, yet the library stood as the city burned. Even when the violence of the Revolution of 1911 saw mobs and armies surrounded the old library, still no damage was done; the walls stood and the books remained safe.

Finally, in 1973, over four hundred years after the library was built, the Red Guard arrived in Ningbo. The Red Guard was an army that hated the past. They wanted only one legend—Mao's legend; and they burned books with the raw eagerness of furious youth. Now Ningbo had many fine artifacts of China's past: monasteries visited by Japanese monks, museums with the great works of Southern painters; but the most glaring symbol of China's past was the old library of Fan Qin, with its wealth of books. The library was the natural target for the Red Guards.

As they gathered in the morning, the waves of Guards grew greater by the hour, and by noon they planned to burn the library to the ground. Now, the Premier of China, Zhou Enlai, heard that the Pavilion was in their sights; but he was in a precarious position. Chairman Mao had cre-

ated the Red Guards, he was intent on destroying the old tales, the old pages and the old legends—and, of course, no one contradicted Mao. But Zhou sent a command. "No book, no scroll, no page, nor image will see the flames of the Guards. The old library of Fan Qin will not be burned." And the angry mob, so dedicated to the fire, turned away.

No one knows why Zhou Enlai risked his life for the books of the Ming collector. No one knows how such a mob could be so quickly parted; and no one knows why—though so many books in China were burned—yet these were spared the fires. But the Library of Fan Qin still stands.

Perhaps, ancient charms, like ancient legends, are true.

PART 3

Mountains of the South

On Receiving My Letter of Termination

The time has come to devote myself to my hiker's stick:

I must have been a Buddhist monk in a former life!

Sick, I see returning home as a kind of pardon.

A stranger here—being fired is like being promoted.

In my cup, thick wine: I get crazy drunk,

Eat my fill, and then stagger up the green mountain.

The southern sect, the northern sect, I've tried them all:

This hermit has his own school of Zen.

Yuan Hongdao (1568-1610), Jonathan Chaves, trans.

Huangshan

The Tiger Fairy

Chen Yuan was a scholar from the province of Zhejiang and, like many a scholar of the Ming, longed to see the wild pinnacles and mist-filled chasms of Mount Huang (*Huangshan*). He had heard of the famous precipices: "Monkey Facing the Sea-Rock," and "The Boulder that Flew in from Nowhere;" and he knew as well of the famous pines and vistas, the cliff-side bridges arching through strange mists, and the lonely paths leading into eerie solitude. Chen determined that he must see these famous sights.

So, taking comfort from the fact that a good map could guide him from place to place, and ashamed that all other artists of note had seen the mountain, and not he, he decided to make the journey himself. After returning from his first post in the capital, he set off for a trip up the Xin'an River from Hangzhou, on to the old town of Tunxi, and then to the base of Mount Huang.

It was late November when he fixed on the day of the climb, but the fine crisp weather at the base foretold an easy day. He spent the morning climbing the steep steps and bridges, as he followed the stone paths and streambeds, hoping as he went that the aspen and gingko might still have some of fall's dazzling yellow. By midday, however, there was a change; blustering winds shook the trees and rain coated the rocks. By mid afternoon, as he sought to descend, a slanting rain dug into his face and he could feel the chill of coming snow. By dusk, he was in the thick of a freezing storm. There was no sign of the little trail he hoped would lead him to the temple. And then, drawing his jacket close about him, he thought he saw a pair of large yellow eyes shining at him out of the dark. Chen hurried on as best he could, following the path down the mountain; but a deep fear gripped his gut.

Suddenly, a little hut seemed to appear out of nowhere; its dark shape outlined faintly against the gathering snow. He could see a small fiery glow shining from the window, and when he touched the door and pressed slowly to open it, he knew he had found shelter.

"My! A Stranger! And look at you! You are soaked," said a stooped little woman with a benign face full of wrinkles. She greeted him with a pat and drew him to the fire.

"Here—let us serve you some hot liquor and some humble snacks," said her kindly husband; and, as they motioned to the little table by the hearth, an exquisite young woman of about sixteen came forward to serve him.

Chen sat down, delighted to feel the warmth from the embers. The old couple's daughter brought out a small dinner and sat to the side as her parents and the guest conversed. By the end of the dinner, only Chen and the girl remained at the table, each one happy in the others' company. Chen was amazed at the girl's manner and conversation. She was guileless and direct—a girl of astonishing charm; and despite the mountain fastness of the hut, she was versed in poetry, like one of those famous courtesans of his hometown. The young woman could compose poems at an instant, knew all the great lyrics the scholars studied for the exams, and had a kind of intelligence and insight that she wore with ease. In just a few hours, with very little trouble on her part, she made the young scholar feel the deep pangs of first love. By the coming of the third watch he was fascinated with her every look and gesture, and by the dawn he knew he had found his life's mate. So, begging to stay longer with the family, he remained a few days; with earnest persuasions, in the brief time, he convinced the old couple of his character and sincerity,

151

and they gave permission for the two to become husband and wife. With prayers to the chasms, rocks and dizzying peaks, and with the strange shaped pines as witnesses, they were married. They remained at the hut for a few days; but then said good-by to the old couple and set off to make a new life in the great world beyond the mountain base.

Chen was a promising young official and so was given a post in the North, where the two settled happily; and though his wife had known no other world than the paths winding through the wild pine trees of Mount Huang, she adapted well to the lanes and shops of the busy walled town. The visits, the festivals, the constant greeting of friends and family, were all natural to her. Indeed, she refused no kindness to those that sought her out and she was known as a willing helpmate to her kinfolk and neighbors. Through all the byways, her tidy house was famous for its well-swept courtyards, fine meals and ready welcome. Eventually she gave birth to two sons and their family was a ranking household in Chen's extended clan.

One day Chen decided they must all return to Mount Huang. "I was so frightened by the storm that I missed seeing the famous sights," he said. "I have heard of 'Monkey Facing the Sea-Rock,' the 'Boulder that Flew in from Nowhere,' and the pine called 'Welcoming Guest;' but I saw none of them. Let's return for a visit. Besides, your kind parents will surely have missed you."

Chen picked a fine week in September when the air was still warm from the summer's heat to spend several days exploring the peaks. The monks of the mountain temples would provide shelter and help them find the paths; and so, the entire family—wife, sons and husband—set off up the mountain. The first day they saw many of the famous sights—the "Refreshing Terrace Rock," and the "Pinnacles of the Eighteen Arhats"—

as they moved among the vertiginous cliffs and ancient pines. But as the days wore on Chen's wife became increasingly preoccupied; the more they walked, and the wilder the views, the more quiet she became.

On the third day, as they all stopped for a rest, Chen saw that his wife had slipped herself way up high onto a great boulder by the side of the path. Her straight back and long black hair were outlined sharply against the sky. She was absolutely motionless, as still as a cat, with her face turned slightly to catch the fine breeze. Finally, as if she could bear it no more, she started weeping.

"What is wrong?" Chen asked his wife. He was overwhelmed by her tears and could not fathom how his happy plan had gone so awry. But she only sat there, in her strange stillness, for some part of the afternoon. As the mid-afternoon sun warmed the rock, something seemed to stir in her; and she chanted a simple poem:

> My hearth, my home, my family sweet;
> Yet my longing for mountains runs so deep.
> Changes of seasons bring fear to my soul,
> That my ancient resolve grows weak.

Chen's wife then looked at him dolefully as if overcome with a terrible regret.

"Come, come!" said Chen Yuan. "This 'longing for mountains …,' this is nothing for my wife to concern herself with. Let us move on to enjoy these amazing sights!"

But his wife remained morose and taciturn, following along as if in a daze. By late afternoon, finally, the family came to the little hut where Chen had first met her. As the two boys sat outside in the sun, Chen and his wife went in to look about. It was completely deserted; dust was everywhere, the little furnishings were broken and no fire had been lit in the fireplace for years.

Listlessly, Chen's wife picked up some old clothes lying in the corner, as if she had lost something. Suddenly, she gave out a burst of laughter full of wild delight. "I didn't know this old thing was still here!" she said, holding up an old tiger skin. There was a gleam in her two bright eyes and she threw the skin over her shoulders. Instantly, as she shook her head, she became a great raging tiger. Her eyes glittered like the yellow eyes Chen had seen in the snow, and her fine stripes rippled as she stretched her huge paws before her. Then, as if in fear at the confines of the tiny hut, she snarled viciously and thrashed and spun about. Catching sight of the door, she made a dash and flew from the hut, rushing past the two boys on the path. Bounding through the pine, she scaled a boulder, jumped nimbly to a cliff, threaded though some rocks, plunged down a chasm and was gone.

Chen ran out of the hut, shaking from the sight of the roaring beast. Calling out to his wife, he clasped his two sons, weeping and sobbing. For days they remained, calling his wife's name from the cliffs. But nothing came back, not even an echo. Chen's wife was never seen again.

Years later, after his sons had taken the examinations and achieved posts in the Imperial Bureaucracy, Chen returned again to find the hut. There were a few traces left, some bits of broken timbers and an old jug for the warmed up wine. Picking up the broken crockery, Chen remembered his wife and their life together. Lost in thought he turned slowly to the door and walked back out into the air; he sat himself down on a rock in the sun and recalled his days as a young official and his life with her and their sons. And what struck him most, as he recalled the past, was not the tidy house and welcoming hearth, nor the affection and love she had shown to their sons, but the sight of her sitting on that steep, high cliff near the top of the mountain, when they had made their return: how still she was on the side of the boulder, quiet as a cat, as if listening to something from far away, with her fine straight back and long black hair outlined sharply against the sky.

Guilin

The Woman Warrior

During the late Qing Dynasty when the Manchu overlords ruled China the government grew fat and corrupt; the Court leeched the wealth of the great trading cities to feed its armies stationed in the west, and starved the Chinese of good governance and good policies. Then, in the floods and famine of the eighteen hundreds, farmers fled to cities that filled with the poor and starving, and internal chaos was ripe. In this terrible time there arose thousands of secret societies. The heroes of these bands of rebels gathered in mountain retreats. Among the caves and strange rock formations they plotted to expel the Manchu from the land of the Han Chinese. One of the most ruthless of these secret societies was called the Triads—the Tian Di Hui—the Society of Heaven and Earth. They gathered warriors and plotted rebellion against the Manchu Emperor in the North. One of their leaders was a woman, called simply, Second Sister Qiu. She came from a poor family in Guizhou; but by the time she died at the age of thirty-one, she commanded an army of over ten thousand.

When she was a young girl, Qiu and her little family survived on what little they could farm, eking out a livelihood as best they could; and when she was fourteen years old, she was married off to a lout from her village. But, with no work, and facing grinding poverty, he soon consoled himself with opium. Second Sister Qiu herself supported the family by helping in a shop that sold bits and pieces of old houses long abandoned by the owners. It was here, among the townspeople, that she saw with her own eyes the venality of the Manchu officials, and like many of the Han race she longed to overthrow the yoke of their control.

One morning, as she was opening up the little shop, a man stood

before her. She noticed right away that he held a string of cash with only three copper coins, and that he had left the third button of his coarse coat undone. Now, though Second Sister was but a young girl, yet she knew what this meant. It was the secret "sign of the three" used by the Society of the Triads. So she wrote in the dust of the street one character. It was simply the word for the Qing Dynasty; but she had changed it by cutting off the top of it. With that change she made the secret sign of rebellion.

The man looked at her directly, "If you are strong and can speak for yourself, leave that opium-addled fool and join us in the caves above Guilin." With barely a glance back to her life in the town, Second Sister left the world of her little village and of her family and joined the army of the Triads.

There she studied the sword, the bow, the cudgel, and the staff, and perfected the breathing exercises and meditation skills to achieve warrior status. She practiced with them for five years and went into battle when she was nineteen years old. Second Sister became famous for her fury in battle and soon she led her own battalion. At the siege of Dongxiangwu she led her force to victory, stunning the soldiers and officers with her brilliance in battle. On her dun horse, with a long sword at her side, she looked like an ancient warrior of the Steppes. She wore the coarse cloth jacket and pants of the archer, but they were embroidered brilliantly in crimson; and she tied her hair up like an opera heroine—in two red silk kerchiefs at the back. In a year she received a larger command, leading a force of more than ten thousand, and in her most brilliant victory she defeated the Manchu army at Tantanxu, where she sent a bitter lesson to the Manchu government. She executed the corrupt officials of the city and opened up the government warehouse for the poor, relieving the famine. Now, throughout the South, everyone knew her name.

But although Second Sister was known as a great soldier and brilliant general, she was still more famous for her speeches. With the bitter memories of her village life, she spoke of what they knew: of the worthless money, the ruined crops and the children abandoned in the streets, of the opium addiction so common among the desperate, of starvation and of humiliation. And Qiu's followers grew day by day. At the head of her Triad battalion, she joined in the conquest of twenty cities along the rivers and canals, and the Manchu overlords grew frightened.

Finally, on her last campaign to the North, in the autumn of 1853, she led her troops against the city of Shilong. But in this town on the riverway, the Manchu had brought their arms and their troops. The Manchu had finally attended to the cities—but not with food or houses or hospitals, but guns. The Manchu fortified the cities with new cannon. Second Sister and her troops were taken by surprise at the siege of Shilong, and in one unified blast of the new cannon, they were turned back. Second Sister Qiu, clad in her crimson costume, fell from her horse and was killed. The Triad armies were forced to disperse—they went underground, melting into the countryside and cities, disappearing until generations later.

Cai Jing and the Sorceress

During the Tang Dynasty there was a young scholar named Cai Jing who studied hard and succeeded brilliantly on the Imperial Examinations, and because of his fine achievement on the examinations, he received an excellent first appointment. Cai Jing served in the Palace itself in the capital of Chang'an.

Every morning Cai Jing arose at dawn and put on his official robes. And Cai Jing loved his official robes. He slid happily into the black jacket of heavy silk, embroidered with the insignia of his department, and took pleasure in gathering the gold threaded damask sash that showed his rank embroidered in red and green, the very high rank of the First Level Attendant-at-the-Right, Tutor to the Imperial Prince.

Cai Jing, however, was more than proud of his appointment; he relished the power, for Cai Jing was a petty man. He enjoyed greatly his Court status, and, indeed, there were no constraints on his arrogance. He oppressed the humble and defied the laws, and after a few short years in office, amassed wealth and goods in great abundance. His greed and his cruelty became known throughout the city.

But because his family was powerful, the Bureau of Rites, which supervised the official class, found it difficult to dismiss him. A direct charge of violating the law was impossible, so his colleagues in the Court solved the problem as they often did; they removed him from the capital. In the tenth year of his service to the Empire, Cai Jing received a new appointment. He was to be sent off to one of the most uncivilized, untamed and barbaric regions of the Empire to serve as local magistrate. They sent him to Guizhou.

In 862, in the middle era of the Tang Dynasty, Cai Jing readied himself for the journey to his outpost assignment. Before his departure, however, he returned home to his family estate to bid farewell to the elders. His family grieved for him: "Guard your health," said his powerful uncle. "The pestilential airs—malaria and plague—are common there. And those natives! They are frightening! Keep far away from their strange practices—those barbarians play the flutes and drums endlessly and the women disport themselves lewdly to make rain and exorcise demons. Do not even look upon these rites! One glance at the black magic of the insect venom called *gu*-poison and you become their ghost-slave forever!"

163

Cai Jing heard these grim words and bowed in gratitude for his uncle's solicitude. Yet Cai Jing was not altogether unhappy. He had heard much about the distant region. People said it was exotic and bizarre. There were dragon monsters and strange creatures that inhabited its famous grottoes, and the eerie rock formations of Guilin. They were, he had heard, "the discarded bones of prehistoric rain serpents." And he certainly knew of Guizhou's wealth. He had seen rich men return from their posts, those who had survived the fevers. They had luggage trains laden with rhinoceros horn, ivory, pearls and shells. But above all, Cai Jing relished the thought of trading in the finest wealth of the region— Guizhou women. Guizhou girls of sixteen brought fine rewards to the Tang entrepreneur. Many went to the Court as dancers—they were famously beautiful and superb at performing the native dances. So with some caution, but with much secret greed, Cai Jing set off for his remote post.

Cai Jing went southward by canal, then by river, through the Nanling mountain range, finally reaching, after weeks of travel, the hot and pestilential land of Guizhou. But Cai found that his arrogant ways served him well in this outpost. He raided the customs offices and treasuries, taxed the local worthies, plundered the coffers of foreign traders, and conscripted the local tribes-people—and through it all, became immensely rich and quite content. Indeed, he hardly thought of the austere northern climate and great Imperial rites he had left behind. Instead, he found that all the wealth of the land—the fruit and fish, fine flowers and aromatics—comforted him greatly.

And now, free of the clan elders, with their annoying frowns of disapproval, Cai Jing indulged his whims unchecked, and he became a great nabob of the region. He expanded the official enclave to create grand boudoirs, theatrical stages and dining halls. He brought to the official residence the native dancers and musicians to perform their lush festival rites, and, despite his uncle's advice, he eagerly gathered the women of Gui to him for his pleasure. And, it seemed, he had no fear of their magic, or of their strange customs. Within a few years, in fact, in his outpost appointment far in the South, Cai Jing was more infamous than he had ever been in the North. And no official, or local worthy, or rich merchant dared correct him.

Yet the arm of the Bureau of Rites is long, and, finally, after Cai had served for seven years in Guizhou, the complaints of the local chiefs, of the traders, and of the families of young girls all reached even to the capital of Chang'an. The Imperial Censors of the Board of Rites reviewed the case. Cai Jing's greed and venality were clear: he had stolen from the Imperial Treasury, executed local chiefs and worthies and outraged the standard of the Bureau with his harem of girls from the countryside. The Bureau of Rites condemned Cai Jing and dispatched an Imperial Envoy to arrest him. But Cai Jing had no desire to return to the capital; he had no intention of returning for punishment. In fact, he had no desire to return for any reason. Those windswept northern winters and dusty summers were tedious to recall; his filial thoughts of his family altars had long departed, and Cai determined to make his escape among the hills and riverways of Guizhou. Somewhere in the tropical growth he would find a tropical village to rule.

Setting off by boat he came first to the merchants from the Southern Islands, but when he sought their help they closed the gates of their dockyards and offices. Then he sought help from the local worthies whom he had taxed and punished, and they stood stony faced before him. Then he pursued help deeper inland among the small villages where he had

found the men he conscripted for labor; but they seemed all to have vanished into the thick forests. Finally, he went to the women by the riverbanks, the women of the strange rites, the women who danced the strange dances, the women he had loved to bring to his estate, the women he had sold to the Empire.

And they welcomed him in.

And Cai Jing was happy. He surveyed the lovely village he came to with a proprietary glance and turned to his servant to bring his luggage forward. The day was blistering hot, at the very beginning of summer on the fifth day of the fifth lunar month. But when Cai looked for his servant to help him settle in, the man who had followed him all this way had disappeared. Yet Cai Jing seemed unconcerned. He was content to stand and watch the women at their magic, content to listen to their eerie ritual. But Cai had arrived at a very sacred time. The fifth day of the fifth month was the only time the women of Guizhou produced their famous *gu*-poison.

As the tropics grew hot and the Double Five Festival arrived, the women of Gui would set out a bowl of water, and dance naked around it, and sing to the God of Medicine. Creeping from the swamps would come the five vilest insects, snakes, and lizards and the women would then capture them, kill them and make them into a terrible poison—a poison that had the power to turn a man into a slave-ghost, a servant for all eternity, subjugated completely, doomed always to carry out the bidding of the women who made the poison—a humble ghost slave for ever. Cai Jing watched eagerly as the women danced in lewd abandonment around the bowl.

Weeks later, with the help of Cai Jing's servant, the Imperial Envoy traced Cai to the little village by the river. As the grave-faced envoy

and his retinue entered the compound, they commanded the women in august tones to reveal Cai's hiding place. They knew he was there; his trunks could be seen in the storehouse. But the women only gave the Northerners a curious look, and continued their work, singing in unison, as was their custom.

The Imperial party was adamant, and they carried out a house-to-house search, and then hunted throughout fields, groves and riverside; they even scoured the caves nearby. Finally, they gave up. They were confounded by the apparent indifference of the locals and could only return home having failed at their mission.

But as they left the compound, they all remarked on the extraordinary tidiness of the village. It seemed more orderly and better stocked than any other they had seen in the South. Every hearth was laid with fresh wood, hundreds of herbs were hung to dry by every gate, and each house had dozens of bright, well-woven, clean garments stacked within. Even the pails and brooms and tools of the village were all set out together in rows.

And of course all remarked on the very tidy piece of silk hanging straight as an arrow on one of the drying racks; there in the sun was the gold threaded damask sash with the red and green insignia of office, that denoted the very high rank of the First Level Attendant-at-the-Right, Tutor to the Imperial Prince of the Tang Imperial Bureaucracy.

The Sea-Toad Immortal

Liang Da was Prime Minister in the Five Dynasties Period, the chaotic era following the Tang Dynasty. He was a man well acquainted with power; he was close to the Emperor himself. He decreed laws and set policy, staffed the bureaucracy with men loyal to him and trained an Imperial Guard to watch over the Court. And though many ministers and even Emperors had fallen in the purges, coups d'état and rebellions of the turbulent times, yet Liang Da survived and thrived. He remained safe in his estate, where he had amassed for himself a great fortune. There he retired each day, protected by his legion of armed followers.

Now, Liang Da was a very devout man. He studied the archaic teachings of Outer Alchemy—the search for longevity through Daoist prescription—and spent long hours in harsh ascetic training and rigorous

meditation exercises. He dedicated endless days to the study of arcane texts, and expended huge sums decocting foul tasting potions; no one in the kingdom was more serious than he. For his tutor in the occult sciences he sought out the most famous recluse in the land, Mountain Recluse Di, to instruct him in the secret grammarye.

Every day the Recluse would be found in Liang's study—appearing as if out of nowhere—to instruct the Prime Minister. This great sage of the mountains set up a rigorous schedule of Daoist exercise, instructing Liang Da in arts of Star Stepping, of Breathing the Cosmic Breath and the strange skill of Achieving a Mystic Sense of Oneness. Now, Liang Da came to rely on his teacher for his penetrating interpretation of the ancient canon and his watchful instruction in the esoteric practices. Every day, when he returned from the meetings in Court he would hasten to his luxurious compound to meet with his teacher. There, in his quiet study far to the back of his fine estate, beyond the clamor of the Court, the two men would unroll the scrolls of talismans and prescription and work through the difficult texts.

One day Liang Da returned from a meeting with his generals; he was eager to get back to the library, to shake the dust of his Court life from his robes in study with his tutor. But the Recluse was nowhere to be found. Liang waited for an hour, sitting expectantly at his desk, but Recluse Di never appeared. Liang became anxious; he sent his servant out to the streets to see if he could find out anything. The servant scoured the town and even the monastery on the hill, but found nothing. The search continued for several hours and Liang Da was beside himself.

Suddenly the kitchen maid came in and said to her master, "Master, that strange man is in the scullery now; we don't know what to do!" Liang hastened back, and, sure enough, there was Recluse Di sitting calmly

at the kitchen worktable, counting the week's supply of eggs that sat in a basket. "We will meet here today," said the Recluse. So they began their discussion of the principles of the Dao, and moved on to the difficult techniques of breathing the Cosmic Breath of the Universe and were about to progress still farther to the topic of Star Stepping, when Liang noticed—as their discussion had progressed—that the Adept had meticulously, slowly, made a tower on the table, a pagoda tower, rising up tier-by-tier, made of coins and eggs—first the coin then the egg, then the coin—on up for twenty-two layers all told.

Liang Da stopped speaking in mid question, and considered the miniature pagoda before him. The eggs and the coins were stacked up to an impossible height—in complete defiance of gravity. Liang sat motionless as he looked at it; he seemed to have been frozen in a moment out of time. A few minutes ticked by, and then an hour. By then, the domestic staff had gathered outside in the courtyard. Finally, as the light in the kitchen diminished, Liang looked up at Mountain Recluse Di.

"Can it all be as fragile as this?" asked Liang Da, quietly.

"Oh no," said his teacher. "Your high command and fine estate, your Palace Guard and stringent laws, are all still more fragile, still more precarious."

"It truly comes down to this?"

The recluse made no reply.

Liang Da nodded, then sighed, then arose from the table. He summoned his servants before him, and paid them a handsome bounty for their good work, giving over his goods to the most loyal. Then he walked from the kitchen, down the fine corridors to the front hall, on through the doors of his estate and out to the hills beyond the town. He took to the life of the Daoist Adept and never again visited the Court, nor any town, nor any great estate, but took to wandering the caves and grottoes that abound in the coastal mountains of the South. On the rare occasions when he was seen by the eyes of man, he was seen with a great, white, ugly, wart-covered sea-toad that draped itself softly over his right shoulder; and so it was that he took as his name in religion, "The Sea-Toad Immortal."

Qu Yuan

They were a terrible race, he thought, given over to lewd rituals, death rites and mid-summer sacrifice—human sacrifice—is what he had been told. Now, of course, they were banned. The Royal House of Chu had driven out their magicians; and their great gods of the rivers and mountains were mere granny tales. The Old Religion was dying out; and it was a good thing, he mused.

Qu Yuan half remembered the stories from his childhood; his old auntie had taught him a few songs from the riverside chants. But now, his mind was elsewhere: on the coming war, the coming cataclysm. He had predicted his state—the great state of Chu, the richest state in the Vertical Alliance—would be engulfed in a war it would lose; Chu would squander its riches and see its young warriors slaughtered. Clearly he was right; but court is not a place for the truth. Court is a place for the lie. "Man is a wolf to man," he muttered to himself.

Qu Yuan had been banished, sent to roam. Once Lord of the Three Wards, Chief Counselor to the King, now he was a cliff-dweller; even the elders of the tiny villages refused him entry—which was exactly to his liking. All comfort grated on his soul. His gut twisted at the fate of his family and his companions, his officers and even his king—his faithless king—who listened to flatterers with their facile lies: go to war, rally the army, victory will be easy. He heard their self-serving counsel fresh in his ears. Of course, the slaughter would be complete. He saw all the deaths as he saw his own: implacable and brutal. "The crossbow was cocked, the bird nets waiting, there was no escape for me," he chanted.

Qu Yuan watched the gathering at the riverside, below the towering cliffs. Those infamous natives—the banned worshippers, the "bar-

Yangtze Gorges

175

barians"—as he had been told as a child—were chanting below, bold as crows, assembled in a chorus of women and men. "Shameless," he thought. The worst of the lot were the magicians—the shaman and shamaness—mad looking in the shaman-madness. They lead a troupe of dancers, all of them snake-like, twisting up and then down: their arms outstretched, elongating, bending, curling and curving. "Demons to summon demons," he thought. He recalled the words of his Confucian teachers. "They are prone to the lewd."

For a moment he thought to upbraid them, to threaten them with magisterial reproofs, when the absurdity of his position came home. "The entangled one," they had called him. Trapped by their lies, then banished, now in miserable solitude. He stood in silence. And, after all, he had to admit, they had survived—in these wild places—among the dizzying cliffs of the Three Gorges. More hardy, he thought ruefully, than the Royal Clan of Chu, soon to be obliterated.

As he started back up the cliff, the full chorus of the shaman-songs reached his ears. The pipes and percussion, the great gongs and chorus of voices filled the air. He gathered his tattered robe around him and sat back into a small ledge. These were strange hymns, he thought, eerie, unlike any of the high court hymns his Confucian teachers had chanted. He edged down the cliff to listen.

"All bathed now in the sweet water scented by orchid—
Our fine hair washed through with perfume.
See us now in silk embroideries—we are flowers.
He is here, come down to us from above. There! He sways.
Such brilliance!—he is radiant before us—

The women were beautiful, dressed to meet the god, singing to call him down, knowing he would meet them and then leave. He had never before heard such doleful beauty in a song. Their sadness was exquisite. He listened for hours, riveted in place, as the rituals stretched on: hymns to the absent god and songs to the fallen: songs of the god's marriage, and the divine drama of god-abandonment. He was captivated by their grief at the separation between man and god.

Above all, the verses stunned him, language he could not have imagined came from their throats. Qu Yuan, the poet once again, stood in rapt attention. How could these unlettered country people, the poor folk of the cliffs and riverside—banned from the elegant training of his childhood—come to such language?

He heard the shamaness invite the River Lord, and the shaman call back the soul; he loved the wild word-play of the divine summons. Lists and noise-words, strange terms and secret charms, naming and renaming, over and over, the sorcerers wrapped their magic in folds of language. And this, he saw, was the shaman's power: to supplant the god's governance: to name with more names than even the gods could know. Then they would fear you; then they would come.

Qu Yuan spent a year by the riverside shrines. Nothing repelled him. He saw the terrible sacrifices and the ecstasy of the dancers; a young girl died at midsummer and an old shaman was burned to cure a drought; and the horror ceased to horrify. He became a faithful acolyte. Every ritual drew him: the marriage to the river god, the mass sung to the fallen warriors, the summoning of the mountain goddess to the divine marriage, the endless dirge to summon the soul, and the great star-stepping journey of the shaman. He fell in with the rhythm of their rites and forgot his old court ways. He became the hermit of the cliffs, a student of the shaman's voice. Descending to their shrines he gathered new chants: month after month, rite after rite. Muttering and humming he took the songs back up to his cave.

And, after all, they took no notice of him.

Soon he forgot the elegant hymns of the court and he sang instead his own shaman-songs. He sang their dirges and elegies, their wild lists and sacred journeys, and filled them with his own grief, gathering his own dark failure to his heart. His doomed state, his foolish ruler and his clan and family, his predictions all unheard, he retold them all in the hard solace of the song. Mad looking and mad-voiced, he took the shaman-sadness to be his own.

His life in the cave was unchanged, even when a few stragglers from the court arrived; four boys, all brothers, escaped from the troubles, struggled up the cliff with an old servant. Like Qu Yuan they were of the Royal Clan, aristocrats who had ran off from the wars, for the great wars had started in earnest. They had the old court ways as well and the eldest could write: taught, like Qu Yuan, by Confucians. They became his scribes, listening to his chants and long narrations. They thought him divine in his mad state, and wrote down all they could catch. Enraptured by the chant he sung, he only stared at them in a kind of furious despond.

Soon, once again, it was time for the Mid-Summer Festival, when the shaman was again sacrificed in the quest of the goddess, when, once again, he would fail in the divine marriage, lament his separation from the goddess and throw himself in the river. Qu Yuan watched the sacred dances and choral hymns that went on for days. Finally, on the morning of the fifth day of the fifth month, he heard the chorus of the Great Death and knew the shaman suicide was immediate. Humming the final verses of his own poem "Encountering Sorrow," he approached the riverside. He wrapped himself in the vines of the cliff and grasped a stone, hug-

ging it to his chest. He plunged into the Miluo River, and died in its surging waters, sacrificed like the ancient shaman of the Old Ways.

The old man was summoned to the court. They found him in the caves above the Three Gorges. He was stooped over and slow of step from both the damp of the cliffs and the weight of his eighty years. Toothless, all he could eat was thin gruel. His clothes were ragged, his hands and feet calloused, yet his delicate ways surprised them. He and his brothers—all the rest now dead—had gone to the cliffs of the Three Gorges as boys. They had remained in hiding for a lifetime. He had never known a world other than the caves and the chants of Qu Yuan. He had been a scribe for the mad poet, and now he was keeper of the scrolls.

The grand officers gathered by the old hermit; they wanted the scrolls. Only he could read the wild words; all the lists of strange names

and sounds. It was the language they needed; it was the language the Emperor had heard of. These were the words once spoken to the gods. What could be a better language for the new Empire of the Han: a conquest empire that would spread its borders the length and breadth of the Sub-Celestial Realm. The clerics bent to every word, copyists at the left and right. Slowly, carefully, the old man repeated the long chants. But he was slow. He stopped in his recitations every hour to take some of the warm rice. But they wanted his poetry the way Qu Yuan had sung it.

The old man continued for days and days, whispering the incantations and fantastic flights, the grief and complaint, the divine summons and death-elegies, working his way through the verses of Qu Yuan. When he finished, the Emperor was pleased, and in gratitude he gave the old man a fine house on the palace grounds; but, of course, he returned to the cliffs. He never learned that the poems he gave them became the

181

court prototypes, the wellspring for the language of the Han court. High praise for the Emperor, accounts of the Imperial hunt or the Imperial park, narratives of visits and travels, eulogies of great men and battles: all were written in the language of Qu Yuan, long dead in the Miluo River, once Lord of the Three Wards of the Great State of Chu.

PART 4

The Earth, the Sun, the Moon

On Hearing of the Death of Matteo Ricci

I read in the Beijing Gazette of the obituary of Matteo Ricci (Li Madou).

Ricci was conversant with many forms of wisdom. He said that the earth and sky together form the shape of a giant egg. The sky resembles the white of the egg, and the earth floats in the sky, just as the yolk floats in the white. He said that there are countries and peoples all over the surface of the yolk-earth in all four directions. The people on the top and the people below stand with their feet directly opposite, just like flies moving about on the beams at the top of a room.

This sounds so strange; but it is just as is foretold in the Sutra of the Scattered Flowers. "Face up, face down, even facing sideways; there are worlds all around us."

Yuan Zhongdao (1570-1623)

The Creation of the World

Long, long ago—even before the time when time itself was counted—the heavens and the earth were a thick and murky soup, called "hundun" or chaos-soup. When all of creation was *hundun*, there were no false distinctions made between strong and weak, fine and crude, smart and stupid, high and low, right and wrong, and no division at all between yourself and others—the perfect state.

But this thick *hundun*-soup changed; the chaos divided, and the murky mix divided into Yin and Yang; *hundun*-soup congealed itself into a viscous liquid-Yin, surrounded by a translucent liquid Yang. It was just like a big chicken egg.

Then a great god was born. Between these two liquids the god Pan Gu emerged, curled up tight in the middle of the *hundun* egg.

Then the egg and the god within mutated. After eighteen thousand years, the egg split apart and became Heaven and Earth; Heaven emerged from the clear Yang liquid of the chaos-egg; and Earth oozed out of the viscous Yin. Then Lord Pan Gu went through nine transformations as he became more divine than heaven, and more wise than earth.

Then the sky and the earth evolved and formed; each day the sky stretched higher by ten feet and each day the earth thickened by ten feet; and as they expanded Pan Gu also stretched and grew: bigger each day by ten feet. After eighteen thousand years, our heavens measured to an immense height, our earth reached to an extreme depth; Pan Gu stood between the two, now grown into a massive giant.

Finally came The Great Transformation. Pan Gu died, and as he died, his body remolded into the world. His breath blew forth as wind and clouds, and his voice rolled out into peals of thunder. His left eye grew

185

hot and brilliant to become the sun above, and his right eye shone down now as the moon.

His arms and legs pushed out and reached afar, to become the four polar, compass-points of the earth, and the five viscera of his body solidified into the five sacred mountains. His blood flowed and formed the rivers, and his veins buckled and reached, stretched and shaped into the ridges and valleys of the land. His flesh and skin lay thick upon the earth and darkened into the rich soil of the fields. The hair from his scalp and beard on his face flew high in the sky and sparkled in the night as stars and constellations, and the fine hair that covered his body took root as grasses and trees.

Then his teeth and bones forged deep into the earth as minerals and metals, the marrow in his bones channeled through the earth as veins of precious stones and jade, and the sweat that flowed on his body soaked the soil of the earth as moisture. Finally, the winds that moved upon the face of the earth stirred the insects and tiny creatures on his body till they stood and walked and talked and looked, and became the black haired people, the first people on earth.

The Goddess of the Sun Xi He

There is an ancient book called *Shan Hai Jing*. It is a road map for monsters. If you follow carefully the directions provided you discover strange creatures and even a few gods, and learn, as well, of the special herbs and magical things that exist in their precincts. According to the book there is not one sun, but ten suns and Xi He, the Goddess, is their mother.

Every day she washes one of her suns until it is nice and clean. As

she rinses it in the cool water just before dawn you can see from far away the steam billowing up from the bath. Then she sets the clean sun up in the great Fu Sang Tree—the Forked Mulberry Tree—and one by one each sun travels the sky, one for each day of the ten-day week. Xi He herself yokes each sun, each day, to her chariot, and drives it across the sky. At the end of the day the Goddess travels below the earth back to the Tree so the sun can rest again in the branches to wait its next turn.

Now, truth be told, the great Confucian clerics of the ancient Zhou Dynasty did not believe in the goddess, but they could not deny the famous myth nor the famous name. So in their accounts of the archaic times, they changed the goddess into a pair of sober mathematicians, a duo of diligent measurers, delimiting and gauging with caliper and compass, the reach of the sun's apparent circuit. The clerics claimed that these two men were sent by the Lord on High to take the length and breadth of the heavens. No more goddess they implied: "And so, the Royal Astronomers Xi and He, at the Lord's command, took to the skies to make fine measurement." So Goddess Xi He who yoked the suns to fly across the sky became, more reasonably, Master Xi and Master He; at least, that's what the Confucian clerics said.

Archer Yi and the the Goddess of the Moon Chang E

Now in the time after the great flood, when Yu the Great had tamed the waters, during the time of the great Xia Kingdom, there was trouble and toil in the Sub-Celestial Realm, and so the Lord on High sent below a great hero named Yi, the Archer. Yi carried the great vermilion bow, with the plain colored arrows and the silk cords, and came to help the people below to save them from the trials they suffered.

One day all the ten suns of the goddess Xi He rose at once in the morning sky and stayed above and scorched the lands. Terrible monsters then arose; the Drought Monster came out of the dry relentless skies, followed by Big Head, the long snake, Giant Face the nine-gullet beast, Cross Brow the dragon-headed beast, and finally, the Great Boar of Mulberry Forest.

So Archer Yi took out his fine bow and arrows and silken cord and shot down all but one of the ten suns and killed as well the monsters of the drought, and saved the people of the Sub-Celestial Realm.

Now Archer Yi wished to obtain the Elixir of Immortality. So he went to the great goddess, the Queen Mother of the West. The Queen Mother gave him the drug, but made him promise never to reveal he had it. But Archer Yi had a wife—the goddess, Chang E—who heard of the drug. One night when the moon was full she stole it from him, and flew away with it to the moon. Though she hid away, the Gods still discovered her crime, and punished her by locking her up on the moon forever. There she remains, as Goddess of the Moon, in her icy palace made of jade. But if you look carefully when the moon is full you can see she is not completely alone. There beside her is a toad, a hare, and a strange old immortal who chops the trunk of a giant cassia tree.

Sources for Stories

Part One: The North

"Guan Yin": Hong Mai, *Yi jian zhi* (Record of the Listener), 12th century.

"The Golden Millet Dream": Li Fang et al., *Wen yuan ying hua*, (Flowers from the Garden of Literature), 10th century.

"White Horse": Oral tradition for White Horse Pagoda (Bai ma ta), Dunhuang region.

"Fan Yuqi and the First Emperor": Sima Qian, *Shi ji* (Records of the Historian), 2nd century B.C.

"The Foreign Monk": Li Fang, et al., *Tai ping guang ji* (Wide Gleanings from the Taiping Era), 10th century.

"Assassination": *Shen zong shi lu* (Veritable Records of Shen Zong's Reign), 17th century, and Zhang Tingyu, *Ming shi*, (Ming Dynastic History), 18th century.

"The Grand Secretary and the Obscene Book": oral tradition.

"The Annoying Ghost": Yuan Mei, *Zi bu yu* (What the Master Does Not Discuss), 18th century.

"Followed by Good Ghosts": Qu You, *Jian deng xin hua* (Tales Told as the Wick Burns Down), 14th century.

"Words in Blood": Li Zhi, *Xu cang shu* (A Book to Be Hidden), 17th century, and Zhang Tingyu, *Ming shi* (Ming Dynastic History), 18th century.

Part Two: Yangtze Delta

"Crazy Ji": *Qian tang hu yin ji dian chan shi yu lu* (The Recorded Sayings of the Recluse from Qiantang Lake, the Chan Master, Crazy Ji), 16th century.

"The Courtesan and the Immortal": Pu Songling, *Liao zhai zhi yi* (Strange Tales from the Make-Do Studio), 18th century.

"Lady White": Feng Menglong, *Gu jin xiao shuo* (Tales Old and New), 17th century.

"The Girl in the Temple": Pu Songling, *Liao zhai zhi yi* (Strange Tales from the Make-Do Studio), 18th century.

"The Garden in the Dream": Qu You, *Jian deng xin hua* (Tales Told as the Wick Burns Down), 14th century.

"Snowy Night": Liu Yiqing, *Shi shuo xin yu* (A New Account of Tales of the World), 5th century.

"The Grandee and the Storyteller": *Min chao dong huan shi shi* (Anon.), 17th century.

"The Fox Wife": oral tradition.

"The Emperor and the Useless Ghosts": *Guo chao xian zhang lei pian* (Imperial Provincial Documents Collected), 16th Century.

"Miao Shan": *Guan yin xiang shan juan* (The Precious Scroll of the Guan Yin of Xiangshan), 18th century.

"The Old Library": oral tradition.

Part Three: Mountains of the South

"The Tiger Fairy": Li Fang, et al., *Tai ping guang ji* (Wide Gleanings from the Taiping Era) 10th century, and Feng Menglong, *Qing shi* (The History of Love), 17th century.

"Cai Jing and the Sorceress": Liu Xu, *Jiu tang shu* (Tang Dynastic History), 10th century.

"The Woman Warrior": *Xun zhou fang zhi* (Gazetteer of Xunzhou County), 19th century.

"The Sea-Toad Immortal": Luo Maodeng, *Sou shen ji* (In Search of the Sacred), 16th century.

"Qu Yuan": Sima Qian, *Shi ji* (Records of the Historian) 2nd century B.C.; *Chu ci* (The Elegies of Chu) Wang Yi commentary, 1st century. Verses from the "Nine Songs" are translated by David Hawkes, *The Songs of the South: An Anthology of Ancient Chinese Poems by Qu Yuan and Other Poets*. New York: Penguin, 1985, p. 109.

Part Four: The Earth, the Sun, the Moon

"The Creation of the World": Xu Cheng, *Wu yun li nian ji* (Chronicle of the Five Cycles of Time) 3rd century, cited in *Yi wen lei ju*, 18th century.

"The Goddess of the Sun Xi He": *Shan hai jing* (Guideways Through Mountains and Seas) c. 2nd century, and Liu An, *Huai nan zi* (Book of Master Huai Nan) 2nd century B.C .; *Shu jing* (Classic of History) c. 4th century B.C.

"Archer Yi and the Goddess of the Moon, Chang E": Liu An, *Huai nan zi* (Book of Master Huai Nan) 2nd century B.C.

The Photographers

Chen Jianxing specializes in the cityscapes and garden studies of Suzhou and the waterside canal towns of the lower Yangtze River. He is president of the Chinese Photographers Association of Suzhou and consultant with the Suzhou Municipal Garden Administration. His work has been extensively reproduced in works dedicated to individual gardens, such as the *The Humble Administrator's Garden*, and in collections of Suzhou photography, such as *Deep Courtyards* and *Famous Gardens of South China*. His book *Celebrated Gardens of Suzhou* is published by China Travel and Tourism Press.

Fang Huazhe specializes in photographing China's sacred mountains as well as ordinary village life. In addition to traveling extensively around China, he has lived in Taiwan, Spain, and the United States.

Li Huixian is chairman of the Guilin Photographers Association. He specializes in photographing the geography of that region.

Li Shaobai specializes in photographing the palaces of Beijing. His work on the Forbidden City has been exhibited worldwide. His work has been published in many books, including *The Mysterious Forbidden City*, *The Great Wall*, *Approaching the Forbidden City* and *The Invisible Forbidden City*.

Luo Tianyou specializes in photographing everyday city scenes in addition to landscapes, gardens, temples, and other significant historical sites in China. He began photographing in 1981. He is also a book editor specializing in publications about Chinese history, art, and culture.

Sun Haibo is the recipient of the "2005 Canon Excellent Photographer" award and was also awarded the bronze medal prize of the 11th International Photographic Art Exhibition by the Chinese Photographers Association. Two of his collections of African photography have been published in China.

Tan Ming specializes in Confucian themes, such as the Confucian Forest and Confucius's birthplace. He has published several collections of his works including: *Shangri-la*, *The Landscape of Tianshan Mountain* and *The Best View in China*. He has exhibited at the British Museum.

Wang Rending is head of the publishing house DeVoyage Books (Daya wenhua chubanshe), Shanghai. He is a professor at Ningbo University and is the director of the Jiangnan Photography Association. His work has been published extensively in photographic studies of the Jiangnan region, such as *Within the Kingdoms of Wu and Yue*. He has also published *The Three Hundred Poems of the Tang, Illustrated with Photographs*. He has edited numerous studies on Chinese cultural history.

Wang Jin is Vice Chairman of the Gansu Province Photographers Association and specializes in images of Gansu, Xinjiang, Inner Mongolia, Sichuan, Tibet, and Yunnan. In 2001, 2003 and 2006 his individual photographic exhibitions were held respectively in Japan, Shanghai and Qinghai Province of China.

Wen Shaojun is Vice Chairman of the Guilin City Photographers Association and is a board member of the Guangxi Zhuang Autonomous Region Photographers Association. Some of his photographic works have been awarded prizes by the 18th National Photographic Exhibition as well as the International Photographic Art Exhibition.

Xiang Xiaoyang is editor in chief of the Chongqing News Association and head of the editorial board of *The People's Daily*, Chongqing Office. He has published multiple books of landscape and architectural photography and has widely published in photography journals. His works include prominent studies of the buildings of the Huizhou World Heritage site, of the lands and peoples of the far western provinces and also of the landscape of Huangshan; he has also published *A Journey to Huizhou*, a photographic and literary account of Huizhou culture.

Yang Dazhou specializes in landscapes, folk life, ancient architecture, and geographic scenes. He has also photographed many temple and hutong scenes. He has published many individual landscape studies such as *The Landscape of the West* and *The Landscape of Bashang*.

Yu Guangming specializes in landscapes, architecture, and microphotographic techniques. Most of his work featured the West Lake in Hangzhou, and many of his collections have been published in China.

Zhang Wang graduated from the National Art Academy of China in 1988 and continued his photography education in the Photography Institute of Beijing Film Academy. His works have been used by more 30 magazines and periodicals at home and abroad. His images taken at the Lingyin Temple complex in Hangzhou were taken during the three years' time he spent in residence there.

Zheng Yunfeng is vice chairman of the Jiangsu Province Photographers Association. He chose the Yangtze River and Yellow River as his main themes, as well as documenting the changes to the Three Gorges region of the Yangtze River, for which he has produced more than 14 books.

Zhou Shimin is a resident of Guilin and specializes in photographing its unique topography, including Shutongshan in nearby Yangshuo City.

Zhu Enguang won the title of "Kodak Outstanding Photographer" in 1998 and was awarded the Golden Statue Prize by the China Photographers Association in 1999. He specializes in natural landscapes.

Photo Credits

Introduction: Sacred Travelers

Wang Rending, Door Ajar

Xiang Xiaoyang, West Lake in Apricot

Xiang Xiaoyang, Road Through Town from Rooftops

Xiang Xiaoyang, The Old Garden

Wang Rending, Windswept Sky

Part One: The North

Luo Tianyou, Ming Tombs in Summer

Xi'an and the Route West

Luo Tianyou, Big Wild Goose Pagoda

Xiang Xiaoyang, Jia Yu Guan Pass

Wang Rending, Bronze Lion's Back, Beijing

Sun Haibo, Statues in Snow, Xi'an

Xiang Xiaoyang, Wet Stone Path

Wang Rending, Sunlight on Doors

Yang Dazhou, Walking in Dust

Li Shaobai, The Great Wall

Yang Dazhou, Green Hillside, Bashang

Yang Dazhou, Soldiers of Qin

Wang Rending, Sand Dunes

Wang Jin, Pasture in Far West

Beijing

Luo Tianyou, Imperial Lion

Li Shaobai, Lattice of Light

Li Shaobai, Light-Dappled Wall

Li Shaobai, Corner Rooftops

Li Shaobai, Moonrise in Forbidden City

Wang Rending, Ancestral Temple, Jiangnan

Li Shaobai, Red Doors

Yang Dazhou, Songbirds

Wang Rending, Light Play on Door, Tianyige, Ningbo

Wang Rending, Hall of Books, Tianyige, Ningbo

Part Three: Mountains of the South

Xiang Xiaoyang, Cliff Face

Huangshan

Xiang Xiaoyang, Mountain Snow

Fang Huazhe, Sea of Clouds

Xiang Xiaoyang, Rooftop View of Tea Shop

Xiang Xiaoyang, Mountain Sunset

Guilin

Luo Tianyou, Li River

Wang Rending, The Antique Shop

Li Huixian, Sky View of Guilin

Xiang Xiaoyang, Carved Hall

Zhou Shimin, River's Edge

Xiang Xiaoyang, Hanging Lanterns

Wang Rending, The Lotus Pond

Xiang Xiaoyang, Dark Inner Courtyard

Yangtze Gorges

Wang Rending, Peach Colored River

Xiang Xiaoyang, Fishing Boats

Zheng Yunfeng, Three Gorges

Part Four: The Earth, the Sun, the Moon

Xiang Xiaoyang, Yunnan Fields

Fang Huazhe, Reeds

Wen Shaojun, Guilin in Pink and Blue

Xiang Xiaoyang, Moon Over Village Pond

Sources for Stories

Chen Jianxiang, Garden Bridge, Suzhou

Opposite

Xiang Xiaoyang, Courtyard with Pony